Writing the City

Writing the City

A Craft Guide to Place, Power, and
the City that Bites Back

Bryan Nyary

Gypsy Press
Chicago

Writing the City
A Craft Guide to Place, Power, and the City that Bites Back

For information, visit Gypsy Press at www.gypsy.press.

Cover photo and author photo by Tae Moon.

Gypsy Press ISBN: 979-8-9995559-0-8
First edition
Library of Congress Control Number: 2025916412

Subjects (Library of Congress headings):
1. Fiction—Authorship.
2. Cities and towns in literature.
3. Urban ecology in literature.
4. Creative writing—Technique.

Creative themes for readers and writers:
‣ Writing cities as characters
‣ Infrastructure and narrative
‣ Movement, memory, and urban transformation
‣ Emotional stakes in the built environment

This book is set in Garamond and Franklin Gothic.

CONTENTS

1

This Is Not Just Setting:
The Problem with Writing Place Flat

Many writing guides treat "setting" like scenery: pick a place, describe it vividly, sprinkle in a few local landmarks for authenticity, then drop your character there and move on. But if you've ever lived in a city—really *lived* there: loved it, hated it, feared it, fought with it—you know that cities don't behave like background.

Cities are not neutral. They are not blank canvases. They are complex, adaptive systems shaped by internal and external pressures. They are restless, self-revising organisms, always becoming something else—rewriting themselves block by block, driven by an evolutionary instinct. They are pressurized environments where memory, class, language, grief, beauty, history, violence, and desire are all stacked—often uncomfortably—on top of each other.

Cities shape you. They mandate how you can move, decide what you fear, influence what you remember, and dictate who you get to become. They hold trauma, contradiction, noise, surveillance, seduction, history, exclusion, and longing. They create their own rules—and if you violate them, they'll bite. Cities gentrify. They collapse. They reinvent. They mark you—and, eventually, they may forget you. They enfold you. They make you negotiate your existence, sometimes street by street.

So why, in fiction, do cities so often feel like afterthoughts? Many novels treat the city as backdrop—a visual reference, a personality shortcut, a proxy for a "vibe." Paris is romantic. New York is fast. Tokyo is neon. Havana is colorful.

Sure, maybe on the surface—or at least in the shorthand of the cultural zeitgeist. But who lives there? Who gets evicted? Who gets anointed—turned into symbol, myth, brand? Who becomes invisible? What does the city want? What does it take? Who does it protect?

These are not scenic details. They are narrative drivers. For fiction set in urban space to live, the city needs to act on its own volition. It needs to have personality, memory, contradictions, agency—and teeth.

This book is about writing the city as a force—not a frame. As a participant—not a passive stage. It's about learning how place can pressure a story, shape character, and carry emotional weight. When a writer treats the city not just as scenery, but as a character, everything in the story can shift—tone, structure, stakes, even plot.

Once the city starts speaking, the rest of the novel has to respond.

City as Character, Not Container

This isn't a guide to worldbuilding or atmospheric description. This is a book about writing the city as a living force in your fiction—one that acts on your characters, resists them, shapes their arcs, and leaves scars. Your city isn't just a container for plot—it's a source of pressure, friction, and change.

This book will help you:

- Make your city emotionally alive—not just a backdrop
- Let geography influence structure, conflict, and pacing
- Write setting as a relationship, not a stage
- Avoid flat, exoticized depictions of "cool" cities
- Treat architecture, memory, language, and infrastructure as narrative tools

Whether you're writing gritty realism, autofiction, literary fantasy, surrealism, or experimental fiction, this guide will show you how to bring urban space to life—and how to let it bite back.

Who This Is For

This book is for:

- ▸ Writers who feel their settings are underdeveloped or interchangeable
- ▸ Writers who have nailed the aesthetic, tone, and mood of place—but want it to carry narrative weight
- ▸ Writers setting stories in cities they love—or cities they fear
- ▸ Writers who want their fiction to engage more deeply with place, memory, and power

You don't need to be an urban planner or geographer. You just need to be curious about how place works—emotionally, structurally, and symbolically—inside story.

What This Book Is (and Isn't)

This is a craft guide, not a textbook. It's voice-driven, direct, and full of practical exercises you can use to rethink scenes or revise your setting with intention. It's short enough to read in a few sittings and deep enough to return to when your draft loses traction and your city feels flat.

What it's not:

- ▸ A guide to nonfiction place writing (though you'll find overlap)
- ▸ A deep dive into urban theory, spatial studies, or urban sociology—but this book draws from theory where it deepens the work, not where it distracts
- ▸ A checklist-heavy manual —this book favors intuition, imagination, and narrative weight over rigid formulas

Instead, it's something in between—a field guide for fiction writers who want their cities to do more than decorate the prose. It's for writers who want their urban setting to act, apply pressure, and mean something.

I reference Chicago often in this book—not as a symbol or backdrop, but out of lived experience. This city shaped me in foundational, lasting ways. It's the city I've lived in and written my way through, where I found love but lost it—where I rescued love, then fumbled and lost it again. I experienced joy and grief on its streets. It's where I built new muscles of resilience and watched others atrophy through defeat and resignation. For years, I moved through the city without fully grasping its influence. Then I began to see that my decisions, relationships, fears—even the shape and rhythm of my days—were being shaped by something larger than me. Infrastructure, spatial boundaries, access, weather, noise, pace, scarcity, social scripts, proximity to power—or erasure by it. All of it working quietly, constantly, invisibly. That realization sits at the core of this book: cities act on people. They affect not just who we become, but how our lives unfold. And the same must be true for fictional characters.

Cities determine the shape of a life, just as they do the shape of a story—its structure, tone, emotional range, stakes, and momentum. They influence character, yes, but also the plotlines those characters are able—or unable—to follow. In each chapter of *Writing the City* I explore a facet of how cities shape narrative emotional texture: memory, spatial inequality, transformation, and time. Along the way, I've included short, practical exercises to help you translate these ideas into your own scenes. Most of my sample answers draw from Chicago—not just because it's familiar, but because it continues to shape how I see, think, and write.

Not Just Setting: Start Here

You don't need to read this book in order, but Chapter 2 lays the foundation: cities have personality. From there, we'll explore structure, rhythm, time, memory, transformation, emotional logic, survival, and ethics. Try the exercises if they're useful—even one can shift how you see place. Once you start writing city as character, something changes. You feel the story in the grid, in the sidewalks, in the wind that channels through buildings. Characters become themselves in the urban setting.

And suddenly, the city isn't just a setting. It's a character. A system. A threat. A question.

Exercise: Your City, Under Pressure

Before we move on, here's one exercise to get you started. Each chapter in this book includes one or more exercises—not to test your skill, but to shift your instincts. These aren't prompts to be perfected. They're designed to help you rethink what cities do in fiction: how they can shape character, pressure plot, and create emotional weight on the page.

This first one is about noticing. Use it to explore how you've been thinking about setting—what a city reveals, conceals, or enforces. You don't need to get it perfect. Just try it. Once you begin to see the city not as a backdrop but as a participant, your writing may start to shift.

Prompt: Think about the city where your current story is set—or, if you're between projects, choose a city you know well. You're going to write about it not as a setting, but as a **force**—something active and shaped by pressure. In a few sentences or a quick paragraph, explore:

- What does this city want?
- What does it resist?
- What does it erase or forget?
- What kinds of people or behaviors does it protect?
- What kinds of people or behaviors does it punish?

Then, try to describe the city as a **character**:

- What is its personality?
- What does it fear or hide?
- How does it seduce, threaten, or test those who live there?

Don't worry about being accurate. Be honest—there is nothing objective about this. These are your impressions of your city—maybe pride, shame, fear, love, frustration, or nostalgia. If you want, let the city become strange, complicated, alive, and contradictory.

(*Optional:* Do this again for the same city at a different time—a different decade, or season, or political moment. What changes? What doesn't?)

5

Sample Answer

Chicago as Force: Chicago wants resilience but punishes softness. It rewards performing—work, hustle, posture—and hides its grief beneath concrete. It resists transparency. It erases its violence with brick restoration and bike lanes. It protects nostalgia, but not memory. It punishes disobedience—most brutally in Black and Brown bodies. If you fall behind, it doesn't look back. It wants you to stay moving. It never wants you to feel too safe.

Chicago as Character: She's charming but suspicious, rough around the edges but strategic. She's always calculating: who you are, where you're from, what side of the grid you belong on. She's seductive in the summer, hostile in the winter, and evasive all year. She remembers everything, even if she pretends she doesn't. She's funny, scarred, and endlessly compartmentalized—but she will not let you forget that you're temporary.

2

The City Has a Temperament

Let's begin with a claim: cities are not passive. They don't just host stories—they animate them. A city isn't simply an aesthetic. It's not wallpaper: charming, decorative, and inert. It's something more integral. Cities might not speak in dialogue or reveal internal thoughts (though you could write them that way), but they move like characters—layered, conflicted, emotionally loaded, and always in motion. And in doing so, they often supply half the narrative engine.

Cities have moods, histories, rhythms, smells, wounds, and desires. They pulse. They brood. They seduce. They scar. They forget. In fiction, they can clarify or distort truth, nurture or destabilize your characters, and act as pressure points that expose deeper tensions.

When I say "write the city as character," I mean: the city should act. It might impose friction. It can distort your protagonist's intentions or whisper possibilities into their loneliness. It can be a collaborator—or antagonist—in your plot's unfolding. A bus that never arrives. A stairwell that smells like home. A corner where shoes are tied before job interviews. A laundromat where confessions come easily. A skyline that makes someone stay one more night. A sidewalk that still remembers the fight. A balcony where no one says what they mean. A park that couples avoid without knowing why—just that it's where things always end.

The City's Temperament

Every city has a temperament. This doesn't mean it behaves predictably—it means it exerts an emotional logic, a psychic climate your characters must navigate. To identify this temperament, don't start with architecture or cuisine. Start with feeling.

Ask:

- What's the emotional weight of this city?
- What does it feel like to arrive here?
- What's it like to wake up here—not just for a day, but every day for twenty years?
- How does it change you over a decade—or undo in a year? What muscles have you had to build, or what has it beat out of you?

Some cities feel on arrival—all neon and momentum—as if you're already behind. Others feel like resignation, where every door is closed before you knock. A city's temperament might show up in the tension between strangers' shoulders on a crowded train, or the way no one makes eye contact at crosswalks. Maybe it's in the daily thunder of jets overhead, or how grocery store cashiers remember your name. Maybe it's the silence in a park that used to be a protest site, or the nervous speed of cyclists dodging sunken manhole covers and glass. Temperament lives in those moments.

When trying to understand a city's temperament, it helps to notice its sensory and emotional contradictions. Try walking without headphones. Take public transit and let yourself simply observe. Sit on a bench at different times of day. Notice how bodies move—who claims space, and who shrinks from it?

Let's ground this with Chicago. Chicago is a city of thresholds—between neighborhoods, between histories, between the visible and the unspoken. Its grandeur lies not just in its lakefront or skyline, but in its contrasts: institutional weight and improvisational grit, Midwestern warmth and structural chill. It's a city that runs on coded language—

how you speak, where you're from, which corner you claim. People who say they're "from Chicago" aren't from Chicago—people who say they live "at Halsted and 33rd" are from Chicago. For many, it rewards resilience; for others, it extracts it. Power moves through its grid in old, often racialized lines, but so does creativity, humor, defiance. Chicago doesn't always explain itself. It watches how you move.

Cities are full of contradictions. Post-hurricane New Orleans might be tender and bruised, yes—but also defiant, pulsing with ancestral music. Certain neighborhoods in Berlin might feel cold and aloof, but others exude subcultural intimacy, slow-burning rage, or queer resilience. Seoul can be relentless, aspirational, but also lonely in its forward drive. Johannesburg may be haunted by injustice, but it's also full of possibility, improvisation, and reclamation. This isn't sociology. Understanding a city doesn't require census data so much as it does curiosity and attention. A city at 7 a.m. on a Monday is a different creature than at 2 a.m. on a Saturday. There's something to hear in both hours.

How to Identify a City's Personality

To write the city as a character, it helps to get to know it—not as a tourist or urban planner, but almost like a psychologist. This isn't about collecting trivia or listing landmarks. It's about attuning to emotional textures, social rhythms, and contradictions. A city's personality rarely reveals itself all at once. It comes in layers.

It often begins with quiet observation. Walking the streets. Watching from a window. Reading local voices. Listening to those who live there. Over time, certain questions begin to surface: What do people tolerate? What do they celebrate—or avoid? What's the unspoken choreography in public spaces—do strangers speak to each other? Do they rush or linger? What's the social protocol for eye contact, deference, smiling? Is there performance in how people dress or posture, or is discretion the rule?

Sometimes a small cue carries meaning: a city where everyone wears headphones might signal emotional insulation. One where people comment on your groceries might signal porousness. A rush-hour train car where everyone stares at their shoes could be politeness. Or exhaustion. Or quiet threat.

Gradually, you might start to notice who's a local and who's not. Not just who lives there, but who *feels* from there. What tells you that? What patterns emerge?

Some cities feel forward-leaning, aspirational, always chasing the future. Others are memory-bound, steeped in nostalgia. Some vibrate with anxiety and fragmentation. Others feel indulgent or theatrical. The emotional climate of a city—its ambient mood—can be just as telling as its weather. Does the place feel coiled with tension on its sidewalks, or does the city exhale?

Questions like these won't offer answers right away. But they begin to surface the city's deeper logic—the kind a story learns to follow:

- What does this city punish?
- What does it reward?
- What kind of person flourishes here—and who fades?

One city might reward boldness—cutting in line, making noise, declaring your ambition. Another might reward endurance—those who don't complain, who keep their heads down and their movements small. One city punishes lateness. Another punishes softness. One erases the past with glass towers; another preserves every brick and calls it progress.

Contradictions are often how a city's personality reveals itself. It might be generous and cruel, soft in summer and brutal in winter. Often, these contradictions show up along lines of class, race, or access. The same street might host a farmers market on Sunday and a food pantry line on Monday. A new coffee shop might serve turmeric lattes next to a payday loan storefront. A plaza filled with children by day might feel unsafe by night. The same city may feel electric to one character and indifferent to another. Those fault lines are worth tracing.

Time shifts a city's behavior. The mood at dawn isn't the same as midnight—during spring thaw compared to peak tourist season. A block on payday Friday is different than on a post-holiday Monday. A city's mood shifts by hour and by season. Try capturing the same block from two different emotional vantage points. You'll notice its temperament isn't fixed—it's reactive. A mural glows in early light, then disappears in winter shadows. A corner might feel jubilant on game night, then tense the morning after. Even snow hits differently depending on who has to shovel it, who has to sleep in it, who has to walk three miles in it to a job they can't afford to lose.

Cities carry memory. Some remember visibly, others prefer reinvention. What does this city recall—and what does it try to forget? Is it still carrying the trauma of a storm, a war, a lost industry, a racial reckoning? Is it haunted by the past or obsessed with reinvention? Some cities leave old bullet holes visible. Others rename everything and pave over the old grid. Some mourn what's gone in murals. Others hide it in glossy development brochures. Some cities bury their grief beneath real estate ads. Others wear it on every street name.

And then there's your own emotional response to the place. How does the city make *you* feel? If you find yourself irritated, overstimulated, charmed, disoriented, threatened, nostalgic, emboldened, cracked open, oddly at peace, or rendered invisible and erased—that's useful data. Your characters will feel it too, in different ways. Let your reaction be a guide, not a verdict.

This isn't about branding—it's about patterns of feeling. Once you begin to sense how a city behaves—what it needs, how it wounds, what it hides—you're no longer writing setting. You're writing relationship.

What the City Reveals—and What it Hides

Writers often begin with the picturesque: landmarks, street food, graffiti. These details matter—but if they don't carry emotional weight, they can flatten narrative. The difference between description and characterization is meaning. Instead of asking *what's here?* ask:

- What part of itself does this city perform, and what part does it conceal?
- What would it be like to grow up here—or to be expelled?
- If this city walked into a room, how would it carry itself?
- What about it would make you fall in love? What would make you leave?

11

A row of neon signs might be just lights—or it might be the way a working-class neighborhood refuses to go dark, even after midnight. A bridge might be a shortcut—or a boundary your character isn't supposed to cross. A mural might be public art—or a cover-up on a shuttered school. The shift is meaningful: from describing what's visible to exploring what it means.

Let's take Chicago:

- **What does it perform and conceal?** Chicago performs strength. It performs hustle, resilience, architectural pride. It shows off its skyline and its lakefront and its sports loyalty with ease. But it conceals its fragility—its segregation, its silences, its aching histories. It doesn't advertise how power has been carved into its neighborhoods or how deeply violence and beauty co-exist in the same block. It hides the way nostalgia and loss are baked into its grid.

- **What would it be like to grow up here, or to be expelled?** Growing up here might mean learning which trains to take and which to avoid—not just for safety, but for social code. It means claiming your block, your high school, your parish, your accent. For some, the city teaches survival through community; for others, through distance. Being expelled from Chicago doesn't always mean exile—it can mean being priced out, over-policed, or ghosted by opportunity. But even then, the city leaves a mark—like a scar you find yourself tracing years later.

- **How would the city carry itself?** If Chicago walked into a room, it would walk in like it had somewhere better to be. Not rude, just distracted. Confident but not performative. It wouldn't smile right away. It would take stock of who's in the room, clock the exits, and keep one ear on the Bulls game. It would offer you a drink—cheap, no frills—and then tell you a story that starts funny and ends gut-punch sad. It wouldn't apologize for it.

▸ **What would make you fall in love, or leave?** You'd fall for the sense of grit and intimacy in its neighborhoods, the way snow can turn a street into a poem. You'd fall for the way strangers hold the door or how a dive bar can feel like sanctuary. But you might leave when the cold stops being bracing and starts being cruel. Or when the grind gets too loud and too long. Or when the city keeps asking you to prove yourself every damn day—and some days, you can't. Or when the enormity, the pace, the noise, the chaos thread themselves into your subconscious and you realize you've been living slightly unnerved for years.

Why We Choose Cities—And What They Choose in Return

Writers often gravitate to cities for their symbolic shorthand. "Detroit is gritty." "Tokyo is futuristic." "Barcelona is sensual." "New Orleans is haunted." These aren't necessarily city personalities—they're marketing tags, cultural projections, aesthetic vibes. There's nothing wrong with choosing a city for its feel. But if the city doesn't alter your character's options, shift the stakes, or impose its own internal logic, it's likely not shaping the narrative.

Try this: imagine your story in a different city. If little would change, you might still be writing *around* place rather than *through* it. A single mom struggling with rent in Boise is not the same as one in San Francisco. A teenage graffiti artist in Atlanta moves through space—and power—very differently than one in Prague. A migrant worker in Houston might have weather and wage on his side but transit and language working against him. These aren't just details. They're story.

That doesn't mean you need to stuff your novel with bus routes and zoning laws. It means the city can shift what's possible. It might warp the story's gravitational field. A character might miss a crucial job interview—not because of bad luck, but because the only bus line that gets them there runs once an hour. A romance might take longer to bloom in a city that rewards guardedness. A romance on shaky ground might not survive in a city where new connections are always within reach—where starting over is easier than staying to repair what's un-raveling. A crime might go unsolved not for lack of witnesses, but be-cause the city taught them where not to look, who not to follow, which stories weren't theirs to tell, and how to stay in their lane.

If you choose a city to suit a story you've already imagined—*My novel takes place over a year and mostly outdoors, so I need somewhere warm. I'll pick Phoenix*—the city risks becoming a logistical backdrop, not a nar-rative force. But fiction rarely thrives on ease. Try flipping the question. Instead of asking, *What city does my story require?* ask: *What story becomes possible in this city?* What tensions emerge in a place that doesn't quite cooperate? Some cities impose limits. They reshape timelines, compli-cate desire, alter mood. They don't just hold the plot—they push against it. Cities are pressure systems. Sometimes, they blow the story off course—and that's where it gets interesting.

Cities Are Emotional Landscapes

In fiction, cities are never just topographies. They're emotional and psychological ecosystems. They influence how time feels, how memory functions, how logic bends—or breaks. A city is more than infrastruc-ture. It's atmosphere. And atmosphere is a form of character.

Cities don't just host feeling—they shape it, amplify it, distort it. Their emotional architecture can compress space, stretch time, or de-stabilize cause and effect. A long block in one city might feel like a gauntlet; in another, it's a breath. A single block might feel endless when you're carrying bad news or vanish in an instant when you're rushing toward someone who might still be there. Fiction that treats the city as a passive backdrop misses the way place behaves as a kind of mood conductor.

Different genres use this to different effect:

- In noir, the city closes in. Streets narrow. Doors lock. Everything drips with unease. The city becomes a char-acter that watches, lurks, withholds. An alley that loops back on itself. A bar where no one looks up. A sound that follows but never overtakes.
- In romance, the city often becomes a site of suspended

14

possibility. Night pulses softer. Cafés glow. A walk home becomes charged with what-ifs. The city blushes—and when love ends, the same street feels abandoned, indifferent. The restaurant sign flickers instead of glows. The bench is wet. The city feels like it's returned to itself and left you behind.

- In literary fiction, the city often reflects interior states. Its weather mirrors anxiety. Its architecture echoes memory. A long walk through a quiet neighborhood becomes an argument with the self. The apartment across the alley glows with the life your character thought they wanted. A garbage truck rumbles past just as they lose their words. The city becomes not just setting, but an emotional double—amplifying what can't be said aloud.

But emotional landscapes aren't limited by genre. A realist novel can make a city feel fragmented, uncanny, or tender by tuning into how characters experience it. A woman walking alone at night doesn't feel the same city as a man heading home after drinks. A child sees different landmarks than a gentrifier. A grieving person notices entirely different details than someone falling in love. To the grieving, every open door feels like a mistake. To the hopeful, even cracked sidewalks shimmer with possibility.

Cities metabolize feeling. That park bench isn't just a bench—it's where she said it, where he didn't come, where something began to fray. A kitchen window isn't just glass—it's how a character watches the world go on without them. A train isn't just transit—it's the engine of leaving, or waiting for someone who never steps off, or something in between. A stairwell isn't just concrete—it's the echo of an argument. A storefront isn't just empty—it's what never opened.

So think of the city not as map, but as moodboard. What textures match your character's inner life? What sounds mirror their agitation or quiet their grief? What places seem to remember them—and which refuse to?

Allow the city to breathe and brood, to echo what your characters can't say, to intervene, to metabolize emotion.

Cities as Mirror, Shelter, Weapon, Ghost

Cities mirror, amplify, distort. They are never disinterested. They shape-shift depending on who enters them—and how they're seen.

A refugee walking through Paris is not moving through the same city as a honeymooning couple. A Black teenager in St. Louis is not in the same city as a White developer breaking ground on a new condo complex. Even within the same novel—or the same day—a city can feel merciful, then punishing. It might open up like a friend or close down like a fortress. Cities perform differently depending on who's watching, and what kind of power—or vulnerability—that watcher holds.

Cities can:

- **Mirror your character's internal state**. A grieving character might perceive a city as gray, emptied out, unkind. The subway platform feels cavernous. A busker sings the song they danced to at their wedding, and it doesn't comfort—it dares them to feel. A billboard shows a face that's gone, and no one around them seems to notice. The same city might appear electric and full of promise to someone falling in love. The same street shimmers. The traffic noise becomes rhythm. A stranger's eyes linger just long enough to suggest possibility. What the city *shows* is shaped by what the character can *see*.

- **Offer shelter—or increase surveillance**. A crowded plaza might feel like anonymity and safety to one character, but exposure and threat to another. To the runaway, the station is a cloak—a place to disappear. To the activist, it's a stage wired for betrayal, every step watched, every shadow recorded. A city might hold out a hand—the library that's always open, the bodega that never asks questions—or put you under a microscope, where every security guard follows, every doorbell camera pings.

- **Bring the past rushing back**. Cities carry memory. A

16

rusted mailbox where letters used to come. A crosswalk where someone was lost. The parking lot where your father taught you how to drive—before he got sick, before you started lying about where you were going. The corner store that used to be a barbershop with his name on the window. The building that survived a fire. The sound of a language you haven't heard since childhood. Cities can resurrect versions of your character they thought they'd buried. Themselves, younger. Themselves, intact.

- **Refract desire, grief, ambition.** Characters project onto the city what they can't yet say out loud. A rooftop garden becomes a metaphor for control. The skyline gleams like a room full of people who won't say your name until you've bled for it. The glass wall of a luxury gym reflects him in a coat two seasons old, carrying groceries that don't quite hide his third-shift fatigue. A boarded-up house becomes the echo of a lost future. A party on a rooftop isn't just a party—it's a glimpse of the life you almost had, if you hadn't left, if you'd been a little braver, if someone had asked you to stay. A graffiti tag isn't just rebellion—it's someone refusing to be forgotten by a city that never said their name in the first place.

Cities are emotional amplifiers, not just locations. They don't simply reflect a mood—they distort and shape it. They can manipulate time (elongating boredom, speeding up danger), shift perception, and even become metaphysical terrain. A memory sharpens at a certain intersection. A betrayal echoes louder in an underpass. A decision feels inevitable just because of the way a hallway bends.

A city might:

- Throw flashing blue lights across your bedroom window when you haven't slept in days
- Bury your timid declaration of love under jackhammers
- Blur your reflection in rain-streaked glass when you

needed to see yourself as real
- ▸ Flash your face across a screen just when you thought no one remembered

This is why writing a city is no different from writing a person. It has memory, personality, attitude, history, secrets. And, like a person, it's not static. What it reveals to one character, it may conceal from another.

To write the city as mirror, shelter, weapon, or ghost is to write it relationally. It's not just about what the city is—but what it becomes when someone moves through it with need, fear, longing, or rage. That transformation *is* the story.

In Summary

Cities aren't just background—they are dramaturgical agents. They shape emotion, dictate tempo, stage conflict, and sometimes steal the scene. And why shouldn't they?

Don't settle for describing your city. Work to reveal its character. Map not just its streets, but its impulses. Consider what it rewards, what it punishes, what it performs, and what it hides. Pay attention to its emotional logic. Let its contradictions sharpen your story's edges. Your story doesn't just take place in a city. It unfolds because of it.

A city can breathe, sweat, scheme, and dream.

Exercise 1: Emotional Cartography

Prompt: Choose a city you've lived in or visited. Without naming landmarks or neighborhoods, map its emotional terrain. Where does anxiety collect? Where does the city exhale? What areas feel theatrical, secretive, seductive, or bruised?

Sample Answer

Anxiety gathers in the blocks where the trains don't connect—on cold platforms in February, on buses that never arrive. The city exhales on stoops in the summer, where kids play with fire hydrants and music blasts from open windows. There's a kind of quiet bruising in the empty lots, the long-closed factories. The city flirts in dive bars with jukeboxes and in half-lit alleyways behind second-floor walkups. There's theater in the protest chants that echo off city hall and in the pride with which people say what block they're from. There's secrecy in the money, in how decisions get made, in which schools survive.

Exercise 2: If the City Spoke

Prompt: Write a monologue from the city's point of view. Give it a voice. What does it think of the people who live in it—all those millions of busy ants it looks down upon? What does it want? What is it tired of?

Sample Answer

"I've watched you grow up on cracked sidewalks and potholed streets. I know the names of your corner stores, your cousins, your heartbreaks. Don't pretend I don't. I hold your secrets in brick and salt. I'm not built for comfort. I'm built for grit. I admire your hustle, but I don't reward softness. I offer loyalty—if you earn it. Shovel your neighbor's walk. Tip your bartender. Don't just photograph me in the Loop and call it love. I'm more than skyline. I'm second-hand bookstores, corner bars, block parties. I'm family reunions in the park, late trains full of possibility. I want loyalty, not flattery. Treat me like a brand, and I'll freeze you out.

You've tried to outpace winter. You can't. Come find me in the alleys, in the snow-packed silence behind a church on Sunday morning. That's where I keep the good stuff. I'm tired of being misunderstood as just cold and hard. I'm watching. I'm waiting. Show me you get it, and I'll fight for you."

Exercise 3: The City in the Room

Prompt: Choose the city your story is set in—real or invented. Now imagine this: you're locked in a windowless room with them for six hours. No phone. No food. No polite escape.

19

Now write:

- What are they like to be around?
- What do they keep talking about?
- How do they try to impress you—or manipulate you?
- How do they make you feel by hour five?
- Do you trust them? Do you want to?

Sample Answer

At first, Chicago's quiet. It doesn't say much. Just sizes me up. There's a lot going on behind the eyes—stories, warnings, pride. After a while, it loosens up, starts talking about high school basketball, labor strikes, house music, the South Side. By hour three, it's pacing. The temperature in the room drops. It tells a joke so good I choke laughing, then turns deadly serious. By hour five, I realize it's testing me—seeing if I'll stick around when it gets uncomfortable. It doesn't trust easily. But it's honest. And that makes me stay.

3

The City That Pushes Back

There's a moment in drafts where I'll ask a writer, "Why is your story set here?" And, often, the answer is something like, "I've always loved New York," or "I needed a city with a subway." Those are good starting points—but they're not the whole picture.

Cities aren't just seasoning. They're infrastructure to stories. When a city actively shapes what a character wants, how they move, or what's possible, it stops being scenery and starts doing narrative work. Again, a test worth trying: If your story could unfold in any other city with minimal changes, you may still be circling around place rather than writing through it.

This chapter is about moving past atmosphere and into architecture. It's about making setting do what good structure always does: apply pressure. A well-written city does more than look good on the page. It constrains and compels, distorts and directs. It creates opportunity for some characters and forecloses it for others. It's a terrain of choices—and consequences.

Some cities have become clichés not because they're overused, but because they're underexplored—reduced to shorthand by stories that reach for mood instead of meaning. Aesthetic detail can start to feel like narrative purpose: neon signs, jazz bars, incense, stray cats. But

21

fiction deepens when those details reveal tension—not just atmosphere. The question isn't "What city feels cool?" It's:

- What demands does this city place on your character?
- What kind of story *has* to happen here—and only here?
- What internal or external conflict becomes unavoidable in this place?
- What does this location force into the open that would stay hidden elsewhere?

When a city is doing its job, it doesn't just host the plot. It shapes it. It changes what's possible—and what's at stake.

How Cities Structure Plot

One of the most powerful ways to use setting is to let it shape your story's architecture. Cities are not just places—they are systems. And those systems govern:

- **Access** – Who gets to enter which spaces? Who can afford to live here? Who feels welcome in the public square, on transit, in institutions? Access is shaped by race, class, language, gender, ability, and immigration status. A gated community, a locked office tower, or a nightclub with a dress code all shape your character's options—and their sense of self.
- **Movement** – How do people move through the city? Are they on foot, by car, by subway, by bike? Are borders porous or patrolled? Is movement fast, dangerous, disorienting, luxurious? Can your character get lost on purpose—or do they have to move through space with precision and caution?
- **Visibility** – Who gets seen? Who can blend in? Who is surveilled, followed, questioned? A city's layout and social norms determine whether your character is exposed or protected, watched or ignored. Think security cameras, unspoken dress codes, streetlight coverage, public affection.

22

- **Conflict** – Where are the lines drawn? Neighborhood boundaries, zoning districts, gang territories, economic divides. Who's crossing those lines? Who's not allowed to? Cities produce friction by stacking different people on top of one another—then drawing sharp lines between them.

- **Timing** – Cities create their own tempos. Think rush hour gridlock, Friday night tension, 2 a.m. loneliness, curfews, public transit schedules, festival season, heat waves, first snowfall. Events unfold differently depending on whether time is compressed, slowed down, or broken apart.

- **Noise** – What can your characters hear? Sirens, neighbors, street preachers, silence. Who gets to be loud? Who has to stay quiet? Acoustic environments affect how people think, act, rest, or react. A noisy city can build pressure. A quiet one can deepen isolation.

- **Resource Distribution** – Where is the nearest hospital? Where do the grocery stores stop? Are there public bathrooms, green spaces, safe housing? Is public transit reliable—or even present? Where can you get prenatal care, Wi-Fi, addiction treatment, clean water? Inequity is spatial. What your character can access—or can't—tells you where the story can go.

- **Ritual and Rhythm** – Cities run on daily, weekly, seasonal routines. School drop-offs, mosque calls, happy hour, car shuffles on snowplow days, street cleaning, tornado siren testing, garbage day. These rhythms set expectations—and disrupt them. They create narrative windows and ruptures.

- **Memory and Legacy** – What's been preserved? What's been erased? Plaques, murals, scars, ruins, repurposed buildings. Cities are layered with history, and that history often ghosts the present. Your character might walk past something that remembers them—even if they've forgotten it.

Here's an example of how the city—and its constraint on movement—shapes emotional consequences when there's only one way through:

> He takes Dearborn Street because he has to—the protected bike lane runs straight through, and the next safest option might as well be a death wish. So every day he pedals through the same corridor of memory, a route paved with lost possibilities, ghosts, and grief. On these blocks, she's in the coffee shop window where she used to wait for him, fogging the glass with her breath. In the patio chair she always pulled out with her bootheel, turning it sideways, coat draped just so. At the bar where she would drink beer and laugh at his jokes. In the door nook where she smoked her cigarettes. He tells himself it's just a commute, but her gravity still pulls him—his eyes flick to these windows without permission. The city has trapped him in her echo. It doesn't matter how fast he pedals. He's orbiting a loss he can't outpace.

Here's a contrasting example—how the city, through access of movement this time, can offer emotional freedom. While one character is trapped in a fixed route through memory, another finds room to rebuild in a different part of the city. Sometimes the city doesn't haunt—it releases.

> She doesn't live near the apartment they shared anymore. She broke the lease and moved across the city right after they split—new neighborhood, new bus line, new skyline through her window. At the wine bar, the bartender only knows her as herself: free, uncoupled, vivid. The café on the corner holds no echoes—just her usual table and the scent of cardamom. She walks different streets, under different trees. No fixed route. No accidental run-ins. The freedom to move—to choose her own direction—is what steadied her. She laughs more. She sleeps better. Her life here isn't a reaction to what came before—it's hers, fully. The city didn't erase the past. It made space for something larger. Movement didn't trap her in memory—it carried her somewhere new.

A good city doesn't just house the plot. It generates it. Cities aren't passive stages; they're pressure systems that reroute, delay, expose, and constrain. When you write into the city's systems, you unlock narrative momentum.

Think about how plot can emerge from:

- **Access** – A character needs a specific medication, but the nearest clinic is across town—and their car just got towed. Or: she wants to visit her son in the ICU but visiting hours don't align with her night-shift schedule—and the hospital won't let her bring her younger kids.

- **Movement** – A transit strike shuts down the trains. Suddenly, your character has to walk through a neighborhood they've avoided for years—and runs into someone they've seriously wronged in the past. Or: construction reroutes traffic, delaying a critical delivery that upends someone's plans.

- **Visibility** – A queer couple hesitates before holding hands in a public park. A formerly incarcerated man enters a courtroom lobby and realizes he's being followed. Or: your protagonist is invisible until they aren't—caught on surveillance footage that goes viral.

- **Conflict** – A new luxury development breaks ground on a block with deep community ties. Protests erupt. A character's loyalties split between their activist roommate and their corporate job. Or: a school rezoning throws rival families into the same district.

- **Timing** – A flash flood shuts down an overpass during rush hour. A blackout turns a rooftop party into a reckoning. A festival clogs the streets just when a character needs to get somewhere fast. Or: a midnight noise ordinance forces a confrontation to end before it's resolved.

- **Noise** – A neighbor's late-night music triggers a PTSD response. Or: a character hears a song from their childhood echoing out of a passing car and follows it—pulling them into a part of the city they haven't seen in years.

25

- **Resource Distribution** – A grocery store closes in a low-income neighborhood. A character's mother now has to take three buses to buy food. Or: a newcomer can't find housing that's affordable and safe, and ends up squatting in an abandoned building where something unexpected unfolds.

- **Ritual and Rhythm** – A Friday prayer service blocks off the street just as a character is racing to deliver bad news. A street sweeper uncovers something someone tried to bury. A character's internal clock begins syncing—or resisting—the city's rhythm.

- **Memory and Legacy** – A developer tears down a family home. In the rubble, a character finds an old letter, sparking a hidden subplot. Or: an old mural gets painted over, and a community erupts in protest. The city doesn't forget—but sometimes, it pretends to.

Each of these city systems can twist your story in unexpected ways—if you allow them to. What starts as a logistical detail can become a turning point.

A city can interfere, block shortcuts, and open trapdoors. It can press against your characters' intentions, reroute their plans, and reveal who they are under pressure. It can force choices they weren't ready to make.

That's what makes a setting matter: not how it looks, but what it demands. Let's see how this plays out in action. What happens when the same character lives in four different American cities?

Case Study: One Story, Four Cities

Premise: A woman discovers a family secret and begins secretly following her father. Same character. Same central tension. But the city reshapes everything: her tools, her risks, her emotional stakes. Set it in:

- **Chicago**: She's following him on foot and by train, weaving through neighborhoods where crossing a block can shift social code. The El is public and exposed; everyone sees everyone. Snow slows everything down. If she loses him in a crowd, she has to wait for the next train—and wonder if it's too late. A slip on ice could change everything. The city demands alertness, toughness, performance.

- ▸ **Los Angeles**: She's trailing him by car, always two vehicles back on the 405. Her surveillance happens at speed—disconnected, distant, sun-glared. Everyone's in motion, and no one walks. She listens to a podcast while waiting for the light to change. The city feels like isolation stretched across miles. When she loses sight of him, she's not even sure what neighborhood she's in. Geography becomes psychological: sprawl as disorientation.

- ▸ **New Orleans**: Narrow streets, unpredictable detours. She follows him past second line parades and boarded-up houses, past ghosts and murals and memories. Her body is close to his. Her breath matches the city's uneven rhythm. At any moment, music or grief could interrupt the trail. Humidity thickens tension. She isn't sure if she's chasing him or the past—or both. The city has seen too much to be surprised.

- ▸ **Washington, D.C.**: Surveillance runs both ways. Cameras are everywhere. Bureaucracy hums in the background. Her father disappears into official buildings, through checkpoints. She can't get in. She waits outside, blending in with interns and aides and protestors. Information is tightly held, and missteps have consequences. Here, power is layered, codified. The story isn't just about what she finds—it's about what she's allowed to know.

Same character. Same plot. But each city doesn't just color the story—it rewrites its DNA. In one version, she's invisible. In another, she's constantly seen. One demands patience, another boldness. In one, the past pulses under the surface; in another, systems obscure everything.

That's how setting becomes story. Of course, not every tension is plot-level. Some of the most powerful frictions come from what a city allows—or refuses to allow.

What's Possible Here? What's Not?

To make a city integral to your story, think in terms of pressure and permission: what does this place make possible—and what does it quietly, or explicitly, forbid?

Every city offers certain freedoms, but they're never universal. One person's freedom is another's risk. One character might walk down the street unnoticed; another might draw attention at every corner. One might find a sanctuary in a crowd; another might feel erased.

Ask:

- **Can your character live openly here, or must they conceal something?** That could mean sexuality, immigration status, mental illness, political views, grief, class background. A city that celebrates openness in one domain might punish it in another. If your protagonist's truth threatens their safety, that tension is story.
- **Are there places your character can't afford, can't enter, can't escape?** Think of gated neighborhoods, luxury lobbies, gentrifying districts, shelters at capacity, social spaces coded for Whiteness or wealth. Geography is never neutral—it tells people where they do or don't belong. When your character pushes against that geography, plot happens.
- **Is the city growing or dying—and how does that affect daily life?** In a booming city, there may be opportunity but also rapid displacement, instability, cultural erasure. In a city in decline, there may be stagnation, unemployment, ghosts of better times. What's rising or crumbling in your setting—and how does that echo your character's own arc?

28

- **What behaviors are sanctioned, and which are punished?** In some places, street vendors are embraced; in others, they're criminalized. Graffiti might be celebrated or erased. A woman yelling in public might be seen as assertive—or unstable. What's permitted in your setting tells you whose stories are legible—and whose are suppressed.

- **What systems operate in the background, and who do they serve?** Think policing, transit, public health, zoning, school districts. These aren't just policies—they're plot engines. A mother might lie about her address to get her child into a better school. A teen might take two buses and a train just to find privacy. These constraints aren't exposition; they're structure.

Place is not just physical—it's psychological, political, and emotional. It invites some characters forward and keeps others on the edge. That interplay—between access and restriction, between visibility and threat—is where real stakes live.

This is especially urgent in stories about identity, trauma, or marginalization. Cities are mirrors, but they're also containers. Some reflect you back, even when you don't want them to. Others refuse to see you at all. Let the city not just shape what your characters can do—but what they *can't*. That's when setting becomes story.

City as Obstacle or Ally

Finally, ask: Is your city helping your character or hurting them? Just as important—when does that shift?

This isn't a fixed binary. Cities are dynamic. So are people. What feels like a sanctuary in Chapter 1 might feel like a trap by Chapter 9. That's not inconsistency—that's arc. Some common turns:

- Maybe the city welcomes them at first—easy commutes, supportive strangers, a sense of belonging. But as they rise in status or visibility, new systems kick in.

Surveillance tightens. Access narrows. A familiar subway becomes a stage. They're no longer anonymous.

- Or maybe the city is indifferent at first—chaotic, impersonal, vast. But something cracks open: a corner store clerk remembers their name, a community forms, a rhythm clicks into place. Suddenly, the city starts offering shelter. Or meaning.

- Or maybe the city doesn't change—but the character does. They grow, regress, unravel. And what once felt like home—like safety, like possibility—becomes unfamiliar. They no longer understand the rules. The music of the place turns discordant.

Let's connect this to the systems that govern city life:

- **Access** – A character who once could walk into any room (a cop, a tech exec, a local celebrity) loses that privilege. They burn a bridge or fall from grace—and suddenly, doors that once opened now stay shut.

- **Movement** – A character recovering from an injury finds the city's inaccessibility newly hostile: subway stairs, narrow sidewalks, broken elevators. A storm floods the underpasses. A rerouted bus line severs their lifeline to work.

- **Visibility** – At first, the character thrives in the anonymity of a big city. Then something shifts—they become a suspect, a whistleblower, a viral face—and now the same streets feel exposed and dangerous. Cameras catch them everywhere.

- **Timing** – A city that once provided structure—reliable trains, steady paychecks—falls into crisis: strikes, blackouts, extreme weather. Now the rhythms are unstable. Every plan risks collapse.

- **Ritual** – A weekly community dinner that grounded your character dissolves due to funding cuts or internal tension. Or: a summer festival that once brought joy becomes a reminder of loss. Ritual turns to rupture.

This kind of relational arc between person and place is one of fiction's most underused. It can be subtle or seismic—what matters is that the city is allowed to change, to reveal new facets over time. Allow that relationship evolve, become dramatic. Let it betray, embrace, or haunt.

Because the truth is: every character has a different city. And every city has its breaking point.

In Summary

Cities aren't just settings. They're systems—with logic, tension, consequence, rules, rhythms, and risks. Allow the city shape the story. Let it press on their vulnerabilities, structure their choices, expand their possibilities—or cut them off.

When the city matters, the story sharpens. The plot tightens. The stakes rise. And the fiction starts to feel not just real—but necessary.

Exercise 1: Match City to Conflict

Prompt: Identify your protagonist's core struggle—maybe they want connection, or power, or freedom.

- ▸ Ask: What kind of city makes that struggle harder?
- ▸ Ask: What kind of city makes that struggle invisible or dangerous?
- ▸ Now ask: What kind of city mirrors that struggle in its own systems?

Write a paragraph describing how your setting either intensifies or protects your character's most vulnerable need. Don't just focus on what the city looks like—focus on how it behaves.

Sample Answer

My protagonist is a queer South Asian teenager trying to hold two versions of himself together: the dutiful son who speaks Gujarati at home, and the boy who rides the Red Line in eyeliner after school. His core struggle is *coherence*—how to be whole in a city that makes him split.

And Chicago is perfect for this, because it's a city built on division: North Side versus South Side, lakefront versus inland, immigrant versus native, Black versus not-Black. He knows which neighborhoods he can walk through holding hands with a boy, and which ones require him to duck his head. He lives in Rogers Park, where every block is a negotiation of race, class, safety, and community.

The train becomes his corridor of becoming: on the train he transforms, in bathrooms at school he hides. The city gives him space to perform, but it also punishes missteps. In Northalsted, he feels like he has to perform a queerness that isn't his. When he's home, he's "too American." Chicago mirrors him—fragmented, tough, coded. It doesn't hate him. It just doesn't explain itself. And that makes him both sharper and more vulnerable.

Here, the city doesn't offer a clean yes or no. It offers a dare: *how much of yourself can you carry without dropping anything?*

Exercise 2: Let the City Intervene

Prompt: Choose a turning point or complication in your story. Then, rewrite that moment to be caused or shaped by the city itself—not just the characters' choices. Make the setting intervene.

Use one of the following systems to drive the change:

- **Access** – a door is locked, a service is denied, a person is refused entry
- **Movement** – a route is blocked, a bus is late, a bridge is out
- **Timing** – a curfew, blackout, festival, or weather event alters the rhythm
- **Visibility** – a character is seen—or hidden—at the wrong moment
- **Conflict** – a boundary gets crossed; a rule gets enforced

Write a short paragraph (4–6 sentences) showing how your city complicates the scene. Let it cause a delay, mistake, reveal, or loss.

Sample Answer

Malik didn't mean to cry on the train. But the text—*"call me"*—landed like a dropped glass, and before he could catch his breath, the train lurched and the lights flickered out. For a second, all he could see was his own face in the window—twisted, wet, trying to hold it in. Someone snorted. Someone else hit record. A girl across the aisle turned to her friend and whispered something that made them both laugh. He was sobbing now—no way to stop it—and the car was too full, too bright, too loud to pretend otherwise. By the time he stepped onto the platform at Jackson, he felt exposed, humiliated. Like the city hadn't just watched him fall apart—it had put him on stage.

4

It's Complicated:
City Versus Character and Character Versus City

Here's a craft truth that applies to both people and place: Every important relationship in a story should be complicated. And one of the most overlooked—and most generative—relationships in fiction could be the one between your character and their city.

This chapter is about relational conflict: not between people, but between person and place. Just like a love interest or rival, the city can challenge, seduce, betray, demand, disappoint, or evolve alongside your protagonist. That's not metaphor—that's structure. When written with intention, the city becomes both pressure system and emotional counterpoint, constantly shaping how your character moves, hides, fights, or changes.

Again, cities aren't neutral. They have rules, rhythms, hierarchies, and histories. Your character may not know them—or may break them deliberately. Either way, that tension creates story.

So in this chapter, we'll ask:

- What kind of relationship does your character have with the city?
- How does the city generate pressure or conflict?

- How does your character disrupt, resist, or alter the place around them?
- And how does that relationship change over time?

When place becomes personal, it becomes powerful. And when a city starts pushing back—or gets pushed—everything sharpens. We get that instinctively with characters—the richest friendships, the messiest romances, the fiercest rivalries are tense, layered, unresolved, never simple. But writers don't always think to apply this same principle to a character's relationship with their city. And yet, when you write the city as character, it's not just there—it's interacting, provoking, seducing, betraying. And your protagonist? They're responding. They might love it. Or hate it. Or love it despite hating it. That dynamic—place versus person, and person versus place—can be one of the most emotionally potent throughlines in a novel.

What's the Nature of Their Relationship?

Imagine your character and your city are in a relationship. What kind would it be? This answer can reveal not just how the character feels about the city, but how the city has shaped their sense of self, their boundaries, their expectations.

Some possibilities:

- **Toxic ex:** The city hurt them, and they can't stop going back.
- **Unrequited love:** They want to belong, but the city keeps them on the outside.
- **Stage parent:** The city demands performance and achievement, constantly pushing them.
- **Estranged family:** They were born here, but don't recognize it anymore.
- **Trauma bond:** They experienced something awful here, and it lingers on every street corner.
- **First love:** They were once enchanted by the city—maybe still are—but they're starting to see its flaws.
- **One-night stand:** The city offered a fleeting thrill, but

no roots, no return.

- **Co-dependent partner:** The character can't function outside the city; the city feeds their ego or their addiction.

- **Long-distance relationship:** They left, but the city still lives in their head. It shapes how they measure every other place.

- **Caretaker dynamic:** They're trying to fix, save, or redeem the city—even if it doesn't want saving.

- **Secret affair:** They hide their true relationship with the city from others—maybe out of shame, maybe out of joy too complicated to explain.

Cities, like people, hold memory. They can wound. They can nurture. And they can trigger past versions of the self. You don't need to explain this dynamic overtly in your story—but letting it inform the writing can deepen what's felt.

The City as Emotional Landscape

When I say a city is an emotional landscape, I mean that it doesn't just reflect mood—it embodies it. A city externalizes your character's inner life, sometimes without their permission. The geography, pace, friction, and sensory experience of a place become expressions of emotion. A character doesn't need to name their grief, for example, if the city they move through *feels* like mourning—cold wind, long shadows, indifferent crowds.

Cities absorb feeling. They metabolize it. They amplify it or flatten it. And just like characters, they hold contradictory emotions—hope and rot, possibility and disappointment, beauty and exhaustion. When your character interacts with the city, they're also interacting with their own memory, fear, longing, and resistance.

Here's how that can play out:

- A character who feels lost might keep encountering dead ends, detours, shuttered windows. The city isn't literally conspiring against them—or maybe it is—but

37

its spatial logic echoes their confusion.

- A character desperate for change may be surrounded by construction noise, demolition sites, scaffolding—visual cues of transformation they haven't accessed yet.
- A lonely character might romanticize the city's grandeur—until they realize no one is looking at them. The scale of the place becomes a kind of quiet punishment.
- A claustrophobic setting—dense apartment buildings, packed trains, overheard conversations—can emotionally crowd a character who's trying to keep a secret.
- A grieving character may walk the same route every day, not for routine but because the landscape hasn't changed—and in that sameness, they find continuity, or pain, or both.

Ask yourself:

- What mood does the city create without dialogue?
- What emotional tone is embedded in the weather, the textures, the light?
- Where does the city resist your character's emotional needs—and where does it surprise them with resonance?

The emotional landscape is not just about aesthetics—it's how place translates feeling into form. A sunny day in a place that feels unsafe creates one kind of tension. A quiet street after betrayal creates another. And a character can misread a city, too—seeing comfort where there's indifference, seeing threat where there's actually care.

Use the city to stage your character's emotional contradictions. Have them love a brutal city. Have them fear a gentle one. Let the emotional landscape say what your character can't.

The City Produces Conflict

Cities are not neutral terrain. They generate friction—culturally, spatially, emotionally. They produce not only external obstacles, but internal destabilization. The city's noise, density, surveillance, pace, and chaos can wear your characters down. Even if the threat isn't visible, the pressure is real.

Think back to the systems outlined in Chapter 2: access, movement, visibility, timing, noise, memory, and the rest. Each of these can become a source of stress, fear, or disorientation. The effect doesn't have to be dramatic. It can be cumulative. Chronic. Grinding.

Here are some of the ways the city generates conflict:

Psychological and Sensory Overload

- **Noise as psychological pressure** – City noise is constant and layered—sirens, shouting, traffic, music bleeding through walls. For a character trying to focus, grieve, or sleep, this can fray their nerves. Backfires trigger old trauma. A neighbor's subwoofer at 2 a.m. becomes the final straw. Even joy can become violence when it's too loud and too close.

- **Crowdedness as surveillance or exposure** – In dense cities, privacy is scarce. Your character is always being watched—or feels like they are. Strangers brush past on buses, stare too long on trains. Small gestures are magnified. A breakdown in public becomes shame. A mistake becomes viral. Even benign attention can feel like a threat when your character wants to disappear.

- **Unpredictability as threat** – Urban systems are never fully stable. Trains delay. Streets close. Power cuts. A protest breaks out without warning. Your character's best-laid plans get scrambled—and they're forced to adapt, reroute, delay, or crack. Control slips through their fingers.

- **Stimulus overload** – City life is an unrelenting barrage of lights, smells, movement, screens, collisions. For neurodivergent characters, traumatized characters, or characters simply on edge, the city doesn't let up. Even pleasure—street music, nightlife, crowds—can feel violent when your character's nervous system is over-taxed.

- **Cultural displacement or erosion** – Your character once belonged here. Now the café speaks a different language, the murals have been painted over, the neighbors have all moved out. This isn't a small change—it's an identity rupture. What happens when your character no longer recognizes the place that shaped them?

Spatial Injustice and Inequity

- **Fragmented geography** – Cities often enforce division through roads, highways, rivers, or zoning laws that keep certain people in—or out. This limits your character's freedom to move, belong, or access opportunity.

- **Infrastructure decay** – Broken elevators, busted streetlights, crumbling public housing—these create friction, delay, and risk. The city becomes both unreliable and unsafe, especially for disabled, elderly, or poor characters.

- **Transit deserts** – A job interview, healthcare appointment, or emergency becomes a high-stakes ordeal because there's no nearby bus route or the trains stop running past a certain hour.

Bureaucracy and Surveillance

- **Red tape** – The city's institutions—schools, courts, hospitals, immigration offices—become sources of tension. Forms are in the wrong language. Office hours conflict with job hours. Your character is made to wait, or is dismissed entirely.

- **Invisibility or hyper-visibility** – Bureaucracy often renders people either invisible (erased from data, planning, care) or too visible (tracked, policed, profiled). Both create narrative pressure.

- **Tech surveillance** – Cameras, facial recognition, predictive policing software—your character might feel watched, criminalized, or algorithmically misjudged.

Economic Pressure

- **Cost of living** – Rent hikes, payday loans, credit card debt—all heighten conflict. Your character might have to choose between paying rent and buying medicine.
- **Gentrification as loss** – Their favorite laundromat is now a juice bar. The soul of their neighborhood is being commodified. Nostalgia curdles into grief, then rage.
- **Multiple jobs, no time** – The city extracts labor. Your character works two jobs and still can't afford rest or joy. Exhaustion becomes a subplot—or a crisis.

Cultural and Symbolic Violence

- **Code-switching** – A character might navigate multiple versions of themselves in different neighborhoods, languages, or subcultures. The city demands constant translation.
- **Erasure** – A character's community isn't represented in signage, maps, media, or political decisions. They see what's missing—and carry the weight of absence.
- **Compulsory performance** – In some cities, your character is expected to be a certain kind of person—hustler, artist, consumer, caregiver. Deviating from that script generates conflict.

Emotional and Existential Disorientation

- **Paralysis by possibility** – The city offers so many choices—partners, careers, identities—that your character can't commit. Abundance becomes anxiety.
- **Alienation in crowds** – Your character is surrounded by people but feels completely disconnected. Loneliness intensifies when it has no room to breathe.

- **Imposter syndrome** – They "made it" to the city—but still feel like a visitor, fraud, or pretender. The city becomes a mirror of their insecurity.

Examples: What This Looks Like on the Page

- **A recovering alcoholic** walks past the same liquor store four times a day because it's the only way to get to work. The city isn't trying to tempt them. But it's built that way.
- **A woman with PTSD** jolts at every siren and backfire. She hasn't slept through the night in weeks. The city sounds like the past.
- **A teenager on the spectrum** is constantly overwhelmed by smells, crowds, sudden noise. He begins skipping school, but can't explain why.
- **An undocumented worker** ducks into alleys when she sees flashing lights—not because she's guilty, but because being seen might end everything.
- **A father trying to hold it together** finally snaps when a garbage truck starts compacting next to his kid's playground and he realizes he hasn't heard silence in six months.
- **A character in grief** tries to find stillness but the city won't allow it. The noise feels cruel, the joy around them obscene. They begin to resent the place, not because it's wrong—but because it won't stop moving.
- **An elderly woman with a walker** waits twenty minutes to cross a major street because the walk signal is too short, and the curb is uneven. When she finally makes it across, she's humiliated and out of breath—but still invisible.
- **A recent immigrant** receives a letter in English from the city's housing office, but can't decipher the warning inside. By the time she finds someone to help translate, her eviction is already scheduled.

- **A single mother** can't attend her child's parent–teacher conference because there's no nearby bus route and she's still waiting on her second shift to end. The city doesn't say "you don't belong"—but its design does.

- **A once-prominent community leader** watches his neighborhood transform around him. Murals painted over. Corner stores gone. He tries to speak up at a zoning meeting—but he's outnumbered, out-funded, and ignored.

- **A young professional in a co-working space** stares at twenty different job tabs on her laptop, unsure of which version of herself to chase. She can become anyone here—and that terrifies her.

- **A queer artist** moves through different scenes in the city, changing how they talk, dress, and walk to fit the code of each space. After a while, they're not sure which version is real—or if any of them are.

- **A Black teenager** is stopped by police while walking home from school—again. Nothing happens, technically. But the city has made its position clear: you're not fully safe anywhere.

- **A trans man** who finally feels like himself in the city's nightlife scene finds that sense of self erode the next morning when the bank teller misgenders him and calls his dead name in a crowded room.

Each of these moments is about friction—between your character and the systems, signals, and social contracts of the city. The conflict may not come from villains, but from design, neglect, or sheer indifference. That pressure can accumulate. It can change your character. It can force decisions they aren't ready to make.

When the city is written as a force that interferes, overwhelms, or ignores, it unlocks a deeper layer of tension—one that's personal, social, and structural all at once.

The city pushes. The character responds. Sometimes they adapt.

Sometimes they unravel. But either way, your setting becomes the external engine of inner pressure. That kind of force can crack their defenses. It can distort their perception.

Because conflict isn't always about antagonists or arguments. Sometimes it's about living in a place that won't let you rest.

A city can do that kind of work. It can wear down your character's coping strategies—and reveal who they are underneath.

The Character Produces Conflict—for the City

But it goes the other way, too. Characters don't just react to the city—they disrupt it. They break its rules, challenge its tempo, refuse its design. They take up space they weren't meant to occupy. They speak when they were expected to stay quiet.

Cities run on a kind of social choreography—unspoken agreements about who belongs where, how fast you move, how loud you are, what you wear, who you love, what you're allowed to ask for. When your character violates those agreements—intentionally or not—they generate friction. Sometimes the city absorbs it. Sometimes it bites back.

Here's how characters can produce conflict *for* the city:

Spatial Disruption

- **A bike messenger** cuts through a closed parade route, sparking a police chase and a media scandal.
- **A sex worker** sets up shop in a luxury district mid-rebrand. Her presence becomes a political flashpoint.
- **A disabled veteran** refuses to move from a broken bus stop until the city installs a bench—day after day, she becomes harder to ignore.

Cultural and Symbolic Resistance

- **A queer teenager** shows up loud and proud in a space that's coded straight—claiming space through visibility.
- **A trans woman** runs for city council in a ward that's

44

never elected someone like her—and forces old power structures to reckon with her presence.

- **An undocumented high schooler** gives a valedictory speech about living in fear, and it goes viral. Her story cracks the city's curated narrative.

Institutional Challenge

- **An immigrant mother** files a lawsuit against a school district that keeps misplacing her child's records. She becomes a symbol of "parental overreach"—but also of survival.
- **A young tenant** organizes their building to resist a corporate buyout. Their protest grows too loud to ignore.
- **A delivery worker** documents unsafe working conditions across multiple boroughs. Their footage calls out not just corporations, but the city's complicity.

Reclaiming the Narrative

- **A street artist** defaces a luxury development billboard with a mural of the families who used to live there.
- **A playwright** stages a guerrilla performance in a transit terminal, turning everyday commuters into witnesses.
- **A community historian** starts sticker-renaming streets—restoring the erased names of women, queer elders, and Indigenous landmarks.

Characters like these don't just live in the city. They agitate it. They refuse to play by the city's rhythms or respect its hierarchies. They bring new meaning to familiar space—or expose the violence beneath the surface.

Your protagonist can become the city's problem—not just its victim. They might disturb the peace, break the algorithm, slow the sidewalk. Because fiction isn't just about surviving a place. It's about changing it—or being changed in the attempt.

This dynamic—city versus character and character versus city—is where the real voltage lives.

The City Has a Will of Its Own

If you're imagining your city as a character, think beyond atmosphere. Consider what it might enforce, what it remembers, what it wants.

Cities, like people, are made of systems. And systems don't like being disrupted. They recalibrate. They retaliate. They have agency. If your protagonist steps out of bounds—crosses a line they weren't supposed to, exposes what was meant to stay hidden—the city doesn't shrug. It notices. And it responds.

Think of the city as having a kind of distributed awareness. It knows what its people are doing—not because it thinks, but because it functions. The transit system logs who tapped in late. The camera sees who lingered too long. The shopkeeper, the neighbor, the parole officer all watch from their own corners. The city has eyes. And when one of its ants moves against the grain, the colony closes in.

The punishment might be immediate:

- A character is arrested for loitering in a neighborhood they used to call home.
- A protestor is hit with unexpected zoning violations.
- A whistleblower's apartment lease mysteriously fails to renew.

Or the punishment might be subtle, psychological, slow-burning:

- A cab never arrives.
- A loan application stalls.
- The lights flicker out just as they reach the elevator.
- They lose their job for "not fitting the culture."

The city doesn't always scream. Sometimes it freezes you out. It offers silence where there used to be sound. Indifference where there used to be attention. Labyrinths where there used to be clear paths.

This is how the city enforces its will—not through dialogue, but through pressure. Not through rage, but through design. The city doesn't throw tantrums. It reroutes trains. It closes doors. It builds new gates and hands the keys to someone else.

Your city can want something—order, containment, obedience, invisibility, silence, loyalty. It might push back when those wants are denied. Because when a character defies the city, the city doesn't just take offense. It takes notes.

And then it takes revenge.

Let the Relationship Change

Just like in any meaningful relationship, a character's bond with the city shouldn't stay static. Cities don't just hold story—they respond to it. And as a protagonist grows, unravels, adapts, or resists, their emotional connection to the place should evolve too.

A city might start as dream, turn into labyrinth, become battleground, and end as mirror. Or the inverse. The change doesn't need to be dramatic, but it should be felt. The relationship between person and place is a narrative in itself.

Here's how that arc might unfold:

- **Beginning:** Your character is in awe. The city dazzles them—its scale, its anonymity, its promise. They feel seduced, like anything is possible. They chase beauty, status, love, reinvention. The city reflects what they want to believe about themselves.

- **Middle:** Friction sets in. The city reveals its cracks—unspoken rules, systems of exclusion, hostile architecture, indifference. What once felt vibrant now feels predatory. Or impersonal. Or simply exhausting. They start to see who gets protected here—and who doesn't. What was once possibility becomes pressure.

- **Climax:** The city demands a choice—or delivers a blow. Maybe it betrays them: a system fails, a secret gets exposed, a loss unfolds in public. Or maybe the city shows up for them in an unexpected way—a stranger helps, a neighborhood rallies, a corner feels like grace. The city becomes the scene of either collapse or breakthrough.

47

- **End:** Your character has changed. So has how they interpret the city. Maybe they leave—finally, with clarity or grief. Maybe they stay, but no longer try to make it love them. Maybe they fight for it now. Maybe they forgive it. Maybe they understand its cost. The streets haven't moved, but something fundamental has shifted.

That change is emotional payoff. It makes the city not just a site of action, but a map of the character's evolution. It makes their growth tactile—visible in how they walk, what they notice, what they mourn, and where they finally choose to stand.

The whole arc doesn't need to be narrated directly. But write as if the relationship is alive—changing, accumulating weight, picking up scars. Because when a character re-reads the city differently than they did before, we know something real has happened.

The city can break their heart. It can teach them limits. It can offer sanctuary just one—and leave them remembering. That's not setting. That's story.

Characters Who Belong and Characters Who Don't

Belonging is one of the most powerful—and painful—narrative engines. It is emotional, cultural, spatial, and sometimes impossible to define. But cities make it visible.

A person's sense of belonging—or their estrangement—is written into geography. It's in which doors open easily, which streets feel safe, who gets a nod on the corner, who gets ignored at the bar, who is always asked, "Where are you from?"

Ask yourself:

- Is your character from this city, or did they arrive recently?
- Do they speak the language—literally, socially, culturally?
- Do they know the references? Understand the codes? Navigate the tempo?

48

- Are they allowed to take up space—or do they have to shrink, defer, apologize?
- Are they trying to blend in, stand out, or take over?
- Does the city accept them, ignore them, tolerate them—or fight back?

Some cities offer instant intimacy—welcoming strangers, embracing difference. Others are slow to trust. They require proof: years lived, losses endured, insider knowledge. And even then, belonging can be provisional. You might feel at home until the rent doubles, until a protest is policed, until a neighbor looks through you. Cities grant belonging—and they also revoke it.

Characters who don't belong carry that tension everywhere. They second-guess themselves on the train. They memorize maps. They overcompensate in conversation. Or they rebel, perform, disappear. The city becomes a mirror of their self-doubt—or a battleground where they try to prove they deserve to stay.

But even characters from the city aren't guaranteed peace. A lifelong resident may find their own neighborhood transformed beyond recognition. Gentrification, displacement, policy changes—all rewrite who the city is for. They might belong historically, but not economically. Culturally, but not legally. Spiritually, but not spatially.

Belonging isn't a static identity. It's a negotiation. A shifting contract. Your story can explore that tension. It can live in micro-moments:

- A character who laughs at a reference too late.
- Someone who lies about their address to get into a better school.
- A woman who changes how she dresses on different sides of town.
- A man who finally feels seen in a space that wasn't built for him.

Belonging is never just about location. It's about recognition. And sometimes, the city doesn't offer it. That tension? That hunger for place, for ease, for home? It's gold. Use it.

In Summary

Cities are not just where your characters live—they're what they respond to, rebel against, fall in love with, flee from, or try to transform. They can challenge your character's values, expose their fears, distort their perception, or tempt them into forgetting who they were.

But cities don't just watch. They respond. They remember. They punish. They evolve. And they often resist being changed.

So think of the city not just as atmosphere but as antagonist. Not just setting, but emotional terrain. Think of it as one of your character's central relationships—maybe even the primary one. It can press, pull, seduce, disappoint. Your characters might fall in and out of love with it. They might try to disappear inside it—or shake something loose within it.

The city can shape your character's arc. And the character can disturb the city in return. Because when place becomes personal, every choice becomes charged.

Conflict deepens. Stakes rise. And story ignites.

Exercise 1: Diagnose the Attachment Style

Prompt: Imagine your character's relationship with the city as an attachment pattern. Is it...?

- **Secure:** They feel grounded, seen, stable here.
- **Anxious:** They obsess over how they're perceived, always seeking approval.
- **Avoidant:** They stay distant. Never commit. Have one foot out the door.
- **Disorganized:** They love it and hate it, feel trapped and obsessed.

Now write two paragraphs—one where your character defends the city to someone who insults it, and one where they confess their secret doubts about it to someone they trust. This tension—between love and ambivalence—is the fuel of good fiction.

Sample Answers

Secure Attachment

To the outsider: "You just don't know her. Chicago isn't about the skyline—it's about the corner stores, the porch conversations, the way people look out for each other even when they act like they don't. Sure, the winter's brutal, but so is anywhere worth loving. This city raised me. I know her flaws. I also know she's the reason I know how to hold my ground."

In confidence: "Sometimes I think I could live somewhere else. Somewhere easier, maybe. But then I'll be on the Red Line, and someone'll give up their seat without making a show of it, or I'll hear house music floating out of a backyard BBQ in July, and I remember—this city's in my blood. I don't always like it. But I trust it."

Anxious Attachment

To the outsider: "You don't get it—Chicago has a rhythm, a code. You just have to try harder. It's not unfriendly—it's just guarded. You have to prove yourself. I mean, yeah, maybe people look through you at first, but once you've earned your spot, it's like nowhere else."

In confidence: "I keep thinking if I just change how I dress, how I talk, what bars I go to—I'll finally feel like I belong. Like I'm not pretending. But the city keeps shifting on me. I want it to love me back. I don't think it does. And I'm tired of trying to guess the rules."

Avoidant Attachment

To the outsider: "Yeah, I love this place. Always have. I know the shortcuts, the best dive bars, which blocks smell like bread in the morning and which ones flood when it rains. I can tell what kind of day it'll be by how the wind feels on LaSalle. But I keep it simple. I'm not trying to fix it or fight it. I stay in my lane. Makes life easier."

In confidence: "I've loved this city my whole life—but when it hurts, I shut down. When the diner closes, when the block changes, when someone gets pushed out—I go quiet. I tell myself it's just the way

51

things go. Because if I let myself feel all of it? The loss, the anger, the helplessness? I'm scared I wouldn't come back from it. So I pull back instead. It's not that I don't care. I care too much. That's the problem."

Disorganized Attachment

To the outsider: "Say what you want—Chicago's real. Unlike half the cities people fawn over. It doesn't fake warmth. It earns it. Yeah, it's harsh. But it's mine. Don't talk shit about it unless you've survived a winter here without complaining."

In confidence: "This city eats at me. I walk through some neighborhoods and feel completely alive. Other days, I can't breathe. It keeps giving me things I love—then ripping them away. I don't know if I'm staying because I love it or because I don't know who I'd be without it."

Exercise 2: City as Mirror or Contrast

Prompt: One powerful way to create tension—or resonance—in your story is to ask: Does the city match who your character is? Or does it challenge them? This exercise explores how your city can function as either a **mirror** (amplifying your character's inner state) or a **contrast** (complicating or destabilizing it).

- Choose one of your main characters. What is their core emotional or psychological state? Are they grieving? Anxious? Disordered? Optimistic? Lost?
- Now ask: What kind of city would reflect that state back at them? (That's a **mirror**.)
- Then ask: What kind of city would resist, ignore, or contradict that state? (That's a **contrast**.)

Write a paragraph exploring what happens when that character is placed in a city that either mirrors or opposes them. Describe how it feels, what frictions emerge, and how this shapes their behavior or decisions.

Example Structure

[Character's emotional state] in *[type of city]* → *Resulting internal or external tension.*

Sample Answer

Chicago as Mirror

A guarded, trauma-hardened woman in a city that doesn't offer softness.
She doesn't ask for help. Neither does Chicago. They both wear their scars like armor. The city rewards her survival instincts—knowing which blocks to avoid, how to disappear into the noise, when to speak and when to keep her head down. She loves the city because it's just like her: proud, scarred, unyielding. No one offers comfort. But when the wind hits right and the El rumbles overhead, she feels seen.

Chicago as Contrast

A grieving, emotionally fragile woman in a city that won't slow down.
Her partner died six months ago. But Chicago doesn't stop. Not for her. Not for anyone. Kids scream on the Blue Line. Street festivals erupt with drums and lights. Her coworkers talk about sports trades and rooftop brunch like nothing happened. She wants silence. Stillness. But the city keeps spinning. There's always another train, another block party, another cop car howling past her window at 3 a.m. And she's not sure if it's keeping her alive—or tearing her further away from what she lost. The city's movement makes her feel forgotten. It doesn't mourn with her. It doesn't pause. And that hurts more than anything.

Exercise 3: Let the City Push Back

Prompt: Your character disrupts something—intentionally or not. How does the city respond? Write a short scene (or internal monologue) in which your character realizes the city is no longer on their side. Maybe they've spoken out, crossed a line, broken a rule—formal or informal. How does the city retaliate? This could be subtle (paperwork disappears), psychological (they stop being greeted), or systemic (services dry up). Show what's lost—and what's revealed.

Sample Answer

She knew the city didn't like her the moment she flinched on day one. A rat darting under a garbage can on Clark, and she screamed—loud. Too loud. A man walking by snorted and said, "Get used to it." But she didn't. She couldn't.

Chicago noticed.

At first, it was small. A rustle near the trash bins behind her apartment. A squeak in the alley outside her yoga studio. A tail slipping out of view just as she turned the corner. But soon it became pattern. The city recalibrated its rhythm around her fear. No matter what block she turned down, the dumpsters seemed to hum. The shadows wriggled. The streets knew.

She wasn't afraid of rats. She was afraid of being undone by them. And the city knew the difference. That was its genius.

She tried walking faster. Avoiding alleys. Noise-cancelling headphones. But the city had her pegged. Every night it offered her a choice: endure it, or leave. And every night, she stayed—shaking, jumpy, unraveling in increments.

Chicago wasn't yelling. It was whispering.

You flinched.

And I remember that.

Exercise 4: Map the Relationship Arc

Prompt: Sketch out the emotional arc of your character's relationship to the city. Label four beats:

- **Initial state** – e.g., awe, alienation, nostalgia
- **Fracture or shift** – e.g., exclusion, disappointment, visibility
- **Climactic choice or reckoning** – e.g., betrayal, rescue, transformation
- **Final stance** – e.g., leaving, staying, reclaiming, accepting

Now write 1–2 lines describing what the city means to them at each point. How has the meaning changed? What's been lost or gained?

Sample Answer

Character: Jalen, 25, aspiring chef, South Side native
Initial state – Loyalty
Chicago is everything. Jalen reps the South Side with pride. He loves the corner joints, the rhythm, the summers that feel like home. He believes the city made him—tough, creative, hungry.

Fracture – Displacement
When his block gets bought up and his family's rent doubles, he realizes the city doesn't love him back. His favorite diner is gone. The faces have changed. He starts to feel like a guest in his own neighborhood.

Climactic reckoning – Betrayal
His pop-up kitchen project gets denied a permit—meanwhile a craft brewery two blocks away gets a glowing write-up and city funding. He sees the game clearly now. It's not about talent. It's about who the city is built to amplify.

Final stance – Defiant belonging
He doesn't leave. But he stops asking for permission. He opens his kitchen in his cousin's garage, under the radar, feeding the people who remember what the neighborhood used to taste like. The city's still his—but now it has to share.

5

Let the City Speak

A lot of writing guides will tell you to "use vivid detail." That's a solid start. But when you're writing the city, detail isn't just about atmosphere or decoration. It's about voice. And voice, at its best, is about point of view, power, memory, mood.

So when I say, "Let the city speak," I don't mean give it lines of dialogue (although hey, go for it if you want). What I'm inviting is something more specific.

Write the city with such specificity, such emotional charge, such sensory clarity, that it feels like it's talking directly to the reader. Whispering. Muttering. Warning. Interrupting. Refusing to be ignored. This isn't description for its own sake—it's about presence.

And that matters—because the way we write cities shapes how we imagine who belongs in them. Writing the city with texture, friction, and voice pushes back against flat representation, aesthetic tourism, and gentrified mythmaking. It reminds us that every block carries history, tension, memory, and power.

Voice Over Visuals

It's easy to confuse atmosphere with emotional resonance. We describe the what—the lights, the sounds, the weather—but forget to embed the why. The result is what we'll call a vibe dump: mood-heavy

57

description with no clear stakes, emotional filter, or narrative pressure. Take this scene:

> The sun slid behind the skyline. Neon buzzed above a bar door. A man smoked outside a liquor store while jazz spilled from a record shop. A dog barked somewhere in the alley.

It paints a picture—but the story doesn't move. The city stays passive. It doesn't tell us how the character feels, or what's at stake. The city is just there—ambient and indifferent. Here's how that same moment could shift if you give it voice:

> The sun dropped fast, as if it didn't want to be part of what came next. Neon flickered overhead—red, then nothing, then red again, its glow unwilling to stay. A man outside the liquor store watched her too long. Jazz spilled out of the record shop, a bright distraction covering something darker. The dog didn't bark—it screamed, and no one stopped it.

Same place. Same elements. But now the scene has voice. It's charged with subtext—implied threat, emotional disorientation, unease. The city isn't passive—it's *participating*. It reflects the character's psychological state. It has tone. It has stakes.

One more example:

> **Flat:** The alley smelled like garbage and wet concrete. Sirens wailed in the distance.

> **Subtextual:** The alley held its breath—rank and damp and watching. Sirens didn't wail. They announced. Like the city was about to choose sides.

In this version, the environment becomes an emotional conduit. Description is no longer just sensory—it's emotionally filtered, shaped by the protagonist's perception, and charged with dramatic implication. That's the power of subtext: when what's left unsaid still alters the emotional pressure in the room.

Think of the city not as a stage, but as an unpredictable roommate—one with its own moods, secrets, and grudges. It doesn't just exist behind the story. It shapes the emotional acoustics of every scene.

So next time you describe the skyline, ask: What is this city trying to say? And why now?

Once you've added emotional subtext, you can take it further: make the world around your character feel lived in, embodied, reactive. That means shifting from surface detail to texture.

Texture Over Fact

It's common to start with the obvious: name a neighborhood, drop a landmark, reference a skyline. Landmarks can anchor a scene—but they're scaffolding, not story. Facts can anchor your setting—but they don't animate it.

Anyone can look up what train runs through a neighborhood or what statue stands in the square. But fiction isn't about what the city has. It's about how the city feels—to this character, in this moment, through the lens of memory, mood, and perception. What you're after is emotional texture: the physical world translated through psychological immediacy. Not a catalog. A pulse. You can ask:

- ▸ What does the air feel like on your teeth when you step outside in February and realize you left your gloves on the radiator?
- ▸ What does the smell under the overpass at noon in July tell you about how long this city lets things rot before responding?
- ▸ What does grief taste like on the #22 bus when your ex boards, doesn't see you, and sits facing the window two rows ahead?
- ▸ What does the rust on a railing say about what this city doesn't have the budget—or the will—to maintain?
- ▸ What does the uneven sidewalk do to a woman in heels who can't afford to be late again?

This isn't about ticking off sensory cures. It's attunement. A kind of sensory-emotional fluency. A willingness to stop observing and, instead, start translating. Your job isn't to tell us what's there. Your job is to tell us what it's like to live inside it. To move through it with fear, hope, and hunger shaping every perception.

Here's the difference:

Flat: The intersection was loud, and the smell of hot dogs filled the air. The Sears Tower rose in the distance.

Textured: The crosswalk blinked as if it was losing patience. The smell of old oil and sweet relish clung to the breeze—familiar, but not comforting. She could see the tower from here, yeah—but it looked smaller than she remembered. The city had pulled away from her, just a little, and wasn't sure she belonged anymore.

The second version isn't more descriptive. It's more attuned. It turns geography into subtext. It lets the city reflect the character's interior world without ever saying it directly. This is the real work of writing place—not describing it, but making it matter.

So: when you write your city, don't just document it. Translate it. Through pressure. Through grief. Through desire, disgust, ambivalence. Through memory and mistake.

The city can touch your character before it touches the reader. Landmarks alone won't do the work—anyone can look those up. What you're after is emotional texture: the city as it's felt, not documented.

The Rhythm of Place

Cities don't just look different—they move differently. Some cities hum. Some groan. Some lurch or stall or glide. The rhythm of a place isn't just ambient—it's architectural. It's embodied. It determines how people talk, walk, stop, collide. And your prose can echo that movement—mirroring the pulse of the city.

Your sentence structure—your pacing, your momentum, your drag or snap or pause—can reflect the city itself. If your city is clipped, fast, impatient, try cutting your syntax. Use fragments. Stack action. Skip the breath.

The train's late. The platform's packed. Someone's yelling. Someone's running. She doesn't flinch. She's already moving—out, down, through, gone.

That's rush hour on the elevated train. That's a block where cars honk before the light turns green. Where a guy jaywalks with a slice of pizza and a wireless earpiece, dodging cabs. A delivery bike buzzes past with a loose chain rattling. A bottle shatters in the alley and no one turns. Someone's yelling into a phone, and somewhere up high, a siren starts to climb. Your sentences can carry that urgency. That torque. That don't-look-back propulsion.

City motion isn't just fast, though—it's patterned.

An El clatters past every six minutes. Traffic lights sync to favor north-south in the morning, east-west in the evening. A bike courier zips between lanes, legs a blur, breath steady. The bus brakes hiss, kneel, open. Doors shudder shut. Move again.

That's rhythm—mechanical, repetitive, urban. You can pace your prose to echo it. Use short, steady clauses. Repeat structures. Vary cadence just slightly, like syncopation in a jazz loop. The rhythm of infrastructure can leak into the rhythm of your sentences.

On the flip side: if your city sprawls or stalls—stretch your syntax. Sentences can drift. They can breathe.

Heat lifts off the sidewalk in ripples. A cicada drones, unseen. Nothing moves but the ceiling fan in the corner bodega, clicking with every slow rotation. She doesn't rush—no one does. Not here. Not now. The air won't let you.

Now you're in New Orleans in July. Or the West Side of Chicago at 2 p.m. in a heat advisory. The rhythm slows. Thought expands. Even tension takes its time. This isn't just stylistic flair—it's tonal architecture. It tells us how the city thinks. How it breathes. And it can shift—not just from city to city, but within a city.

- Chicago at 8 a.m. in February isn't Chicago at 2 a.m. in August.
- Rush hour is all elbows and escalators.
- Midnight is glacial—blue lights, snow hush, salt trucks passing like ghosts.
- Sunday morning limps—trash skitters in the wind, buses crawl half-empty, and grief waits at the light.

Even the same place changes depending on who's there:

- A 19-year-old biking deliveries through Wicker Park in July writes in speed.
- A retired woman on her porch in Bronzeville might write in loops, in memory, in pause.
- A street medic in a protest march downtown on a Friday night writes in fragments—surge, hold, run, don't look back.

Your prose can adapt—by neighborhood, time of day, season, weather, emotional state, public noise level, internal chaos. The movement of the city can shape the momentum of your language.

So when you write the city, ask:

- Where is the tension accumulating?
- How does this block move?
- What's the dominant rhythm here—stop-and-go, smooth flow, jittery chaos?
- Should this sentence slam forward, or hold its breath?

Every city speaks in tempo. The work is to listen. Then write to the beat of its breath.

The City Speaks in Sound

Writers often go visual-first. They tell us what a city looks like. Skylines, signage, silhouettes. But that's not how cities announce themselves.

Cities speak in sound first.

Before you see the street, you hear it—the hydraulic hiss of a bus kneeling, the low growl of a motorcycle jumping a light, the speaker on a stoop blasting bachata or drill, the El screeching metal on metal as it rounds the curve at Wabash and Van Buren, the doppler warble of a siren heading north on State, the single sharp horn from a cab that wasn't actually in danger—just annoyed. A bottle rolls into a gutter. A man coughs hard and spits. A door buzzes and no one answers. Somewhere, a bird is trapped in a vent, its small body in panic—wings slapping against steel, wild, rhythmic, wrong.

Sound doesn't wait to be noticed. It arrives. It forces its way in. And it's often how we know we're still in the city.

When sound alters mood

A car alarm bleats. No one checks. It just becomes part of the rhythm—like a minor key under the melody of her thoughts.

A baby cries in a second-floor walk-up and doesn't stop. The dog in the apartment down the hall is yipping incessantly, has been for hours. Someone's yelling three blocks over. She can't make out the words, just the shape of them. And it's enough.

Sound creates geography—both real and psychological. You know where you are by what you hear:

- The chick-chick of a crosswalk button.
- The gasp of a train pulling in under the platform.
- The clang of a Metra train bell as it pulls into Lasalle St. Station.
- The high, pained buzz of a streetlight on its last life.
- A basketball thudding rhythmically against cracked pavement in a fenced lot behind a corner store.
- The slap of flip-flops and the jingle of keys as someone runs late.
- A sudden squawk of walkie-talkies from a cluster of cops outside the bodega.
- Laughter that turns too sharp and too fast, and then cuts off entirely.

When sound cuts in

It can crack a moment open. It can shift the emotional register or drag a memory to the surface.

- A funeral home shares a wall with a daycare. There's a kind of mercy in how the laughter leaks through.

- A woman rehearses opera in her garage every Sunday. The street slows to listen—then speeds back up.
- A dog howls every time the Blue Line rattles overhead. Your character finds it comforting. Like someone else is also tired of pretending.
- An ambulance passes. She holds her breath without meaning to. Not out of fear. Out of habit.
- A sudden metallic crash—like a trash can, or a fight. Or both. She looks up and forgets what she was feeling.
- A voice breaks into song on the fire escape. Beautiful. Off-key. Unapologetic. It's funny until it's not. Until the voice cracks into something raw.

Summer in Chicago is loud

Everyone's windows are open. The ice cream truck plays a melody so distorted it feels ironic. A man is DJing from his porch like the whole block is his dance floor. Someone's power-drilling something at 10:30 p.m. and no one's stopping them. A group of teens bounces a speaker in a shopping cart, bass turned all the way up. Fireworks crack at all hours, no holiday in sight. A neighbor sneezes seven times in a row. The city replies with a single "Bless you!" shouted from somewhere unseen. The train passes. Again. Then again. You don't get silence here—you get rhythm. And rhythm is memory.

When silence speaks

What isn't said often arrives through what is heard. A slammed door. A muttered threat. A silence that follows a noise that should have kept going.

The street outside goes still—too still. No train. No bus. No shouting. She knows something's wrong, even if she can't name it yet.

The apartment next door is usually loud. Tonight, it's quiet. A chair scrapes once—then nothing.

Sound is one of the city's primary languages. It's how the city announces, insists, bleeds, celebrates, warns. If your city goes quiet, make sure that silence means something. That it signals rupture—not just absence.

Quick Sound Prompts

- What's the first thing your character hears when they wake up?
- What noise repeats so often they've stopped noticing it—but shouldn't?
- What sound breaks the mood of the moment?
- What rhythm marks this block, this season, this hour?

Sound belongs in your scenes. It can interrupt. Echo through alleys and apartment walls. It can shape your character's nervous system, whether they notice it or not. Because a city isn't a silent backdrop. It talks. Constantly. And your reader deserves to hear it.

When the City Speaks in Syntax

Cities don't just speak—they argue. They overlap, interrupt, layer themselves in competing rhythms and dialects. A single block might hold five languages before noon. Spanish on the corner. English in the bank. Yoruba in the beauty supply store. Polish at the bus stop. Silence at home. What's spoken isn't the only thing that matters—what echoes, lingers, or slips into the grain of a sentence matters too. City language doesn't stop at the edge of dialogue. It infiltrates narration. Mood. Memory. Thought.

A narrator's voice might shift depending on the block they're walking, or the emotional register they're in. A protest chant or a preacher's cadence might slip into their interior monologue and stay there, echoing. They might describe a corner like it's a warning label. Or a prayer. Or an ad.

City language—its syntax, rhythm, accent, silence—can shape your prose from the inside out. Not as performance, but as texture. That might mean a line shaped like a subway announcement: clipped, impersonal, slightly delayed. *Attention passengers. All service is suspended due to an earlier incident. We apologize. We always apologize.* It might mean a paragraph that starts like a billboard—*Now Leasing. Luxury Living*—and ends in an internal voice that knows the difference between promise and reality. *She's three months behind and sleeping on her sister's couch. Nothing about this feels like luxury.*

The way your characters think can reflect the city's influence. A kid raised on text threads might write their own life in fast, clipped fragments—underpunctuated, mood-first. A character raised in a church tradition might think in anaphora, with rhythm and call-and-response built into their logic. A line might unspool like gossip, or flatten into public-service language. Even silence can be communicative. *She said nothing. Not even a mmm. Just looked at him like she was watching weather happen—nothing to stop, nothing to fix.*

Urban voice is fluid, and fiction can honor that. Cities don't speak in one register—they speak in collisions. You don't need to push it hard. But if you listen closely, the city's language will start writing your sentences for you. It'll shape the rhythm of your narration. It'll tell you when to sharpen, when to blur, when to slip from exterior to interior voice without a seam.

That can happen on its own. Prose can code-switch when the city does. It can argue. It can overlap. It can sing.

Reading the Walls

Cities speak through visual residue. Not just in what they build, but in what they patch, cover, label, ignore. Language gets scrawled, printed, taped, carved, projected. Some of it official. Some of it urgent. Some of it unsanctioned but deeply sincere.

A mural appears on a corner—then gets painted over. Then reappears. A flyer for a missing person fades on a light pole, curling in the humidity. A bathroom stall in a club becomes an open letter, passed back and forth in marker and pen: someone writes *He*, someone else crosses it out and writes *They*. Someone adds a heart. A transit poster says *See Something, Say Something*, and someone's written *Yeah, Okay* underneath.

These aren't just visual details. They're commentary. Micro-dialogues. Power plays. Leftovers from a fight someone didn't win. Or didn't finish. Walk into a neighborhood and you can read its priorities on the walls.

- A boarded-up window tagged with *Stop Shooting. Start Living.*
- A rusted *Out of Order* sign zip-tied to a broken elevator that hasn't moved since March.
- A *We Call Police* sign in a store window two blocks from a mural that says *No Cops. No Jails. No Borders.*
- A wheelchair ramp chained off with a handwritten sign: *Sorry. Use back door (if open).*

Infrastructure is political. Graffiti is dialogue. Signage is mood. Every visible element of the city has the potential to reflect—and pressure—your characters. Maybe they notice. Maybe they don't. Either choice tells us something.

> She sees the fresh paint on the corner wall—same shade as the housing authority's truck. Someone covered the faces again. She keeps walking.

> He notices the sticker on a sign pole: *Housing Is a Human Right.* It's peeling at the corner. He presses it back down without thinking. Holds his hand there a second too long.

Visual language often arrives in layers. A city doesn't erase; it accretes. What's painted over never fully disappears. And what remains tells you what the city tolerates, what it can't afford to fix, what it pretends not to see.

On wooden poles and weathered walls, posters accumulate like sediment: punk shows stapled over lost cat flyers, tutoring ads obscuring mutual aid callouts, rent strike info half-torn beneath a poetry night. Services, sorrow, survival—all thumbtacked and taped to the same battered surfaces. Rain warps the paper, the sun bleaches the ink, but the voices remain. Each new sheet doesn't replace the last—it presses down on it, like memory layered under time.

This kind of residue belongs in fiction:

- A train car with overlapping ads—cosmetic surgery above a crisis hotline.

- A cracked sign at the entrance of a shuttered school: *Excellence. Equity. Safety.*
- A bus shelter tagged with a phone number and the words *Call for help*, no explanation.
- A faded tow zone sign that everyone ignores because the city does, too.
- A community garden locked with rusted chains, sprouting weeds through gravel.
- A playground mural of smiling children half-obscured by gang tags and water damage.
- A hand-lettered *We're Hiring!* sign in the window of a business that closed months ago.

This isn't just world-building. It's character-building. What your protagonist sees, what they register, what they filter out—all of it reveals where they're from, what they've learned to pay attention to, what they're trying not to feel.

A city's built language is never neutral. It tells you who has power, who's being watched, what's being sold, and what's being resisted. It's everywhere—on billboards, in broken signs, in public service announcements, on protest posters wheat-pasted to brick. On stickers on bathroom mirrors. On sidewalks in chalk.

Even the train speaks. *Belmont is Next. Doors open on the left at Belmont. Transfer to Red and Brown Line trains at Belmont.* That official language can enter your narration, too—especially when it clashes with what your character is experiencing. The PA says, *Thank you for riding the CTA,* but your character is bleeding. Or afraid. Or watching someone get escorted off in cuffs. That tension? That's narrative energy.

Visual language surrounds us. Don't just describe it. Let it say something. Because what the city puts in front of us—on purpose or by accident—isn't just backdrop. It's a living transcript of the place and its priorities. And in fiction, every sign is a potential signal.

The Uneven City

Cities don't speak to everyone the same way.

Some neighborhoods whisper. Others shout. Some offer shade,

quiet, and choice. Others blast noise, limit options, and surveil movement. These differences aren't aesthetic—they're structural. And they leave a mark.

To write a city with voice, ask: Whose voice is this? Whose version of the city are we in?

A block that gets its trash picked up daily has a different tone than one where rats run the alleys. A character who's never seen a foreclosure notice has a different internal rhythm than one who crosses the street to avoid the city marshal. A three-minute walk from the train in one ZIP code might mean crossing six lanes of traffic and two vacant lots in another. A character who never waits more than five minutes for a bus lives in a different city than someone who needs two transfers and an hour to cross town. One hears birds. The other hears sirens. One lives on a block that gets plowed first. The other hasn't seen salt since last Tuesday.

These aren't just socioeconomic facts—they're narrative pressures that shape voice, pacing, and perception. They can shape the tone. They can shape urgency. They can shape what your characters believe about what's possible. Because where you are in a city—what's nearby, what's missing, what's broken, what's policed—shapes how you move, how you speak, and how you're heard.

Spatial inequality isn't just background—it's tone. It's tempo. It's emotional resonance.

Your character's experience of the city—their pace, their filter, their sense of danger or delight—is shaped by what the city gives them, and what it withholds.

Some stories flatten this complexity. The city becomes any-city, the grit stylized, the hardship ornamental. But if you're trying to write a city that speaks, the listening has to include power—who holds it, who lacks it, and where it hides.

- Where is investment concentrated?
- Where is it withheld?
- Where are the trees, and where are the sirens?
- Who lives near greenspace—and who lives under expressways?
- Where are the working streetlights—and where are

69

they always out?

- Who gets corner stores, and who gets liquor stores?
- Where are the cameras, and who are they watching?
- Who gets gunshot detectors, and who gets silence?
- Whose streets get plowed first in winter?
- Where are the wheelchair ramps—or the stairs with no railings?
- Who gets protected bike lanes, and who dodges traffic and potholes?
- Where are there public bathrooms—and who gets locked out?
- Where are the rats, and where are the gardens?

Those disparities can shape what the city sounds like. Smells like. Feels like. Inequality doesn't just exist in the background—it moves through syntax, stakes, subtext. Writing the city isn't just about capturing its energy. It's about honoring its fractures.

Cities aren't built on even ground. Every block reflects a different story about power—what gets funded, what gets policed, what gets ignored. Be careful not to flatten those distinctions. Let them pulse through your fiction. Because spatial inequality doesn't just shape the city's surface. It shapes who your characters believe they are—and what they believe they deserve.

Who Gets to Move

If cities speak, then they do so in motion. But that motion isn't available to everyone in the same way—or at the same cost.

Cities promise movement. But they don't offer it equally. Some characters flow through the city. Others are delayed, diverted, stopped. Movement itself becomes a kind of language—one that communicates who's welcome, who's suspect, who belongs, and who's being tolerated. And your prose can reflect that.

This is more than logistics. It's point of view. It's texture. It's narrative charge.

A character in a car writes with distance—seeing the city in aerial glimpses, through speed and glass. A character on a late bus writes

70

from fatigue and observation, full of ambient noise, shared space, and delay. A cyclist feels torque, proximity, risk. A person pushing a stroller, carrying groceries, moving through the city with chronic pain or invisible trauma sees not just terrain, but resistance. That resistance can shape tone.

A smooth commute isn't just convenience—it's privilege. A stalled train isn't just an inconvenience—it's exposure. A shortcut through a quiet block isn't just a time-saver—it's a gamble, depending on who you are and what hour it is. A late bus isn't just a delay—it's a risk missed, a shift lost, a reason to be questioned. A locked building door isn't just security—it's a line between welcome and suspicion. And a long walk home isn't just distance—it's vigilance, reroutes, keys between fingers.

Mobility Is Voice. And Restriction Is Tone.

Does your character walk fast to pass as someone who belongs? Do they avoid certain neighborhoods—not because of fear, but memory? Do they stop, stall, double back—not because they're lost, but because they've learned to make space for someone else's comfort?

These choices aren't just character details. They're how the city speaks through your character's body. They determine the rhythm of the prose. The urgency of a line. The emotional acoustics of a scene.

Some learn to shorten their stride in wealthier neighborhoods—not to appear in a rush. Others keep their heads down near flashing lights—not out of guilt, but survival instinct. Movement becomes code-switching: posture, speed, and silence adjusted like dialect.

Access isn't just about transit. It's about legibility, safety, and permission. It's about who gets to move without being questioned—and who has to justify their presence at every turn. When you write movement in the city—walking, biking, riding, waiting—consider it more than mechanical choreography. The fastest route isn't always the most revealing. A path can bend under history. It can detour through fear. Stall under pressure. Or be interrupted by the city itself.

Mobility becomes subtext. Friction becomes voice. Because in fiction, how a character moves tells us how the city sees them. And that, too, is the city speaking.

Hostile Design and the Language of Space

Cities don't just speak through signs or sound. They speak through space.

The layout of a sidewalk. The angle of a bench. The presence—or absence—of shade, shelter, seating. These are not neutral design decisions. They're acts of messaging. Of control. Of quiet enforcement. Every tree planted or not planted, every security camera mounted, every curb ramp preserved or removed, every unlit underpass or over-bright plaza is saying something: about who's welcome, and who's not.

This is where environmental design becomes power. Especially in the form of what we call hostile architecture: design choices made to displace, deter, or erase—without ever raising a voice.

You've seen it, even if you didn't notice:

- **Anti-homeless benches** – Public benches segmented by metal bars or angled forward to prevent lying down or sleeping.
- **Spiked or textured deterrents** – Concrete or metal features (e.g., spikes, bumps, ridges) placed on flat surfaces to discourage sitting or lying down.
- **Sloped ledges and planters** – Angled or curved surfaces that look decorative but are designed to prevent resting.
- **Urine deflector panels** – Angled corner shields that bounce liquid back at the source, used to discourage public urination.
- **Blue lighting** – Installed in public bathrooms or tunnels to make veins harder to find, deterring intravenous drug use.
- **Timed sprinklers** – Set to go off late at night or during off-hours, not for watering, but to keep people from sleeping nearby.
- **"Mosquito" sound devices** – Emit high-frequency noise that only teenagers and young adults can hear, used to deter loitering.

- **Sonic deterrence through classical music** – Speakers play loud classical music (often Mozart or Vivaldi) on a loop—pleasant for passersby, but disruptive enough to prevent lingering or sleep.
- **Rock beds and boulder fields** – Decorative-looking stone placements under overpasses or in unused green space, meant to prevent tents or encampments.
- **No-back or split-seat benches** – Designed to discourage comfort and prevent lying down while waiting for transit or rest.
- **Underpass lighting removal** – A tactic that increases threat and disorientation at night while claiming to discourage crime or encampment.

These are not accidents, they're policies disguised as form. And fiction can show this—not just as detail, but as friction, subtext, pressure. A character's relationship to a space reveals how the city sees them—and what it's trying to make them feel. You can show that tension through the design itself. Here are a few scenes built from refusal and friction:

The Bench: She used to sit here after work, nursing a sandwich and ten minutes of quiet before the bus. Now the benches tilt forward like they're trying to throw people off. No backs. No rest. She doesn't sit anymore. Just paces the curb, waiting, exposed.

The Curb Cut: He used to roll up the sidewalk with ease, but the curb cut's gone now—replaced by a raised bed of concrete and petunias. Decorative, they said. Preventative. He bumps his chair twice before giving up and circling to the alley, swallowing the burn in his arms.

The Alley: He ducked into the alley like always, aiming for the corner that stayed dry. But the city installed angled tiles that push back—slick and sharp, designed to shame. He turns away midstream, soaked and furious. The wall answered first.

The Soundtrack: She used to sleep behind the convenience store— quiet, hidden, safer than most. Now Mozart blares on a loop, crisp and constant, all night. It's not the volume that gets her. It's the way the violins feel like laughter, like a dare to stay still.

The Sprinklers: He stretched out behind the church steps—flat concrete, clean enough. At 3:08 a.m., the sprinklers hit. Ice-cold and deliberate. The first shot got his feet. The next got his spine. He didn't move right away. Just lay there, blinking up at the stars, knowing damn well it wasn't about the landscaping.

The Boulders: She limped toward the old spot under the viaduct—where they used to leave socks, a water jug, notes taped to the pillar. But now it's all boulders. Not decorative. Not natural. Just inhospitable. A landscaped no. She sat anyway, shoulder to stone, head to knees, pretending it didn't hurt.

This is the city speaking. Not in dialogue, not in monologue—but in design. In constraint. In refusal. And the truth is: some people don't notice. Because the space was built for them. The bench supports their posture. The train stop is accessible. The lights feel safe. The space works. That's the power of design that reinforces privilege—it disappears. It feels "normal."

But if you want to write a city that breathes, that argues, that insists—it has to include who gets to rest, and who doesn't. Who's protected, and who's removed. Because built space is never passive. It regulates behavior, emotional access, bodily safety. It signals who belongs—and who's meant to keep moving.

When you write city scenes, go beyond what a space looks. Ask:

- Who can rest here?
- Who's watched here?
- What behavior is this space trying to permit—or punish?
- What's missing?

Even the most subtle piece of infrastructure carries tone. A bench that's too short. A transit stop with no cover. A fence too low to be security, too high to be art. These aren't just background features. They're emotional architecture. They shape mood. They produce stakes.

Fiction can reflect that pressure. Characters might react—visibly or not—to the way a space is designed to reject them. They might find ways around it. Internalize it. Fight it. Or simply adapt, without even noticing when or how.

Sometimes the city doesn't need to say no—your character has already learned to stop asking. Because cities don't just express power through laws or police. They express power through design that pretends not to be political. And fiction that writes the city as neutral is missing the story.

In Summary

To write a city that speaks, think beyond scenery. Start hearing the city as a presence—with rhythm, with rules, with pressure.

Cities don't just sit there. They argue. They loop. They regulate. They exclude. They shift tone by time of day, by ZIP code, by body. They speak in rust, in signage, in broken elevators, in sirens that come faster to some blocks than others.

Fiction can respond to that pressure—on the level of the sentence, the image, the beat. You can tune your sentences to the city's emotional, structural, and political pitch:

- Your prose can move like the El—mechanical, erratic, rhythmic.
- It can reflect speed, delay, detour—what access feels like on foot, on wheels, in fear, in memory.
- Sound can interrupt, signage accuse, syntax echo mood.
- Benches, curbs, cameras, and barriers can shape what's possible.
- Friction can tell you whose version of the city you're writing.

Because cities aren't just settings. They're collaborators. They shape tone, pace, and stakes. They speak—in texture, in tempo, in design, in refusal. They reshape your character's body in space. Fiction can carry both the city's noise and its quiet violence. Not just what the city looks like—but what it means, what it withholds, what it demands. Not flat. Not neutral. But charged. And speaking.

Exercises 1: Describe a Rainstorm Without the Word "Rain"

Prompt: Write a 200-word passage set during a rainstorm in your city. Don't use the word "rain" or any generic weather terms (storm, wet, gray, drizzle, etc.)

Focus only on what the city does in response. Questions to guide you:

- What do gutters say?
- How do windows behave?
- What sound happens on subway stairs?
- What does the city smell like?
- What does traffic do?

Treat the environment like a character with a secret, and watch how it reacts.

Sample Answer

The gutters gagged first. A slick bubbling noise, like someone trying not to choke. She watched a plastic bottle spin in the eddy near the curb, then disappear. A siren wailed half a mile away—then cut short, like it decided to turn back. Shoes slapped faster against sidewalk. Coats turned into shields. On the stairs down to the Blue Line, someone slipped and swore, loud. She didn't look up. Just gripped the rail and descended like the walls were closing in. The air smelled like metal and sour heat, like the city had finally admitted something shameful. Inside the station, a puddle formed under the map of the train lines. The Blue Line was delayed. The speaker stuttered, clicked. Then silence.

Exercise 2: Translate a Block's Rhythm into Syntax

Prompt: Pick a specific block at a specific time of day. (Rush hour? Late night? Sunday morning?) Write a paragraph where the sentence structure mirrors the pace and mood of that moment.

- **Fast** = clipped, breathless, stacked clauses.
- **Slow** = long, winding, sensory-heavy.
- **Uneven** = stutters, fragments, starts and stops.

Sample Answer

(Mid-morning, midweek. Uneven tempo—half-rush, half-rest.)

A jogger passes. Then a stroller. Then two women with coffee, talking over each other about childcare and salary bands. The light turns green. Nobody moves. A man in a Cubs hoodie waves someone through. The dog next to him barks once. Silence again. She adjusts her bag. Crosses the street. Keeps going.

Exercise 3: Use Found Language

Prompt: Write a short scene in which your character interacts with found city language—a sign, mural, sticker, graffiti, billboard, subway announcement, etc. Let it shift the mood or reveal something about what they're avoiding, remembering, or afraid of.

Sample Answer

She passed the mural on the viaduct without reading it—until she didn't. Until the third time that week, when her eyes caught the bottom corner: *You are not a lost cause.* It looked hand-painted, added later. The letters were smaller than the rest. A different color. Almost smudged. She stood there a beat too long. Someone brushed past her. "You good?" She nodded. She wasn't.

Exercise 4: Let Sound Interrupt

Prompt: Write a moment where sound interrupts your character's thought, conversation, or emotional trajectory. Let it shift the tone or reveal contrast between their inner world and their surroundings.

Sample Answer

He was halfway through explaining why he hadn't called when the train screamed overhead. Not passed—*screamed.* Metal on metal. A shriek. Neither of them spoke. The sound took its time, like it knew it had the right. When it finally faded, he looked down at his coffee. "You were saying?" she asked, but he had nothing left.

Exercise 5: Write the Barrier

Prompt: Choose one piece of hostile architecture—a bench with dividers, spikes on a ledge, anti-homeless sound deterrents, a blocked-off public bathroom, etc.

Now write a short scene (150–200 words) in which your protagonist encounters that object and is affected by it. Focus not just on the physical logistics of the disruption, but on how the character responds emotionally, improvises, detours, or breaks down in its presence. Ask:

- What were they trying to do?
- What's being denied?
- How do they explain this denial to themselves?
- Do they internalize it, resist it, accept it?

Imagine the object speaks first. The city resists—not loudly, but through design. Not with cruelty, but with indifference. Then show us how the character responds.

Sample Answer

He turned the corner blind, legs burning, lungs high and tight in his chest. Didn't look back. Didn't know if they were still behind him. Just ran.

The street spit him out into a plaza—too bright, too exposed. But there, near the bus shelter, was a bench. Metal. Long. Empty.

He stumbled toward it, heart ragged, ready to fold. But the seat was curved like a slide, tilted forward like it didn't want him. Three steel bars split it into awkward wedges. No back. No lean. No room to collapse.

He tried anyway. Sat sideways, knees crooked, arms clutching his ribs like they might fall out. His skin buzzed. His breath skipped. The bar dug into his spine.

He couldn't stay. Couldn't breathe.

Across the plaza, a man walked a dog without looking at him. A camera blinked above the ATM. A horn sounded—close. He stood, dizzy, too soon.

He ran again. This time slower. Not by choice.

6

Plot Lives in the Map

I f your story could just as easily unfold in a coastal town or mountain retreat, the city might not be pulling its weight. Urban space shouldn't just host the narrative—it should pressure it, distort it, restrict it, transform it. Geography shapes what's possible, heightens tension, collapses timelines, and keeps resolution just out of reach.

Where your characters go, how they get there, what that movement costs or reveals—these aren't background details. They're story. Not extra. Not decorative. The map *is* the plot.

Turning the City into Structure

This chapter is about how urban structure can become narrative structure. Cities are designed spaces—zoned, gridded, carved into corridors, choke points, and detours. But that logic isn't just physical. It's emotional. It's political. It's craft.

Writers are often taught to plot stories chronologically: what happens first, next, and last. But cities invite a different lens—one rooted in space. What happens where? How hard is it to get there? Who belongs in that space, and who doesn't? What do the walls, lights, traffic, or exits say about what can unfold?

Characters don't just move through the plot. They move through the city. And the city pushes. This chapter looks at how you might:

- Use the city's geography to shape dramatic beats
- Let movement through space build structure and suspense
- Treat boundaries, zones, and planning decisions as plot devices
- Build narrative rhythm through repetition and detour
- Borrow structural logics from real cities—train lines, zoning grids, vertical access, gentrification flow

Each of these choices shapes what's possible—because a conversation on a park bench has different stakes than one under a flickering streetlight outside a shuttered bodega. Setting amplifies or muffles what's happening. Tune into how your city is built, and you'll start to hear scenes differently—charged with tension, location, and pressure.

Spatial Structures as Plot Forms

Cities create natural narrative tension. They're built for friction—of bodies, traffic, cultures, systems. Every corner, corridor, and crossroads can trap, delay, expose, or pressure a character.

Looking for claustrophobia? Send your character underground—into a stalled train, a boiler room, or a service tunnel. Want to invoke paranoia? Set them on a crowded bus or a rush-hour platform where no one makes eye contact. Craving intimacy? Move them to an alley behind a club, where sound bleeds but no one watches. For disorientation, try a gridless neighborhood or an intersection where every direction looks familiar—but none of them feel safe.

Urban space offers countless narrative levers. You might:

- Shut down the subway line just as time runs out
- Remove cell service in an underground garage
- Block exits with a protest or parade
- Redirect your character through an unfamiliar or dangerous neighborhood
- Force them to wait in a space that is surveilled but abandoned

Geography doesn't just frame outcomes—it alters them. If your protagonist has to cross the city to stop something from happening, then traffic, surveillance, class boundaries, police checkpoints, zoning laws, broken elevators, weather, and fear all become antagonists. Plot can emerge not from what a character wants—but from obstruction and how hard the city makes it to get there.

A character might know where they need to go. But the city doesn't care. The express train skips their stop. The street is blocked. The shortcut is gentrified, and they no longer know anyone behind the doors. The city becomes a second antagonist—not through malice, but through indifference. And that, too, is a kind of pressure.

Boundaries as Plot Devices

Cities are built on borders. Some are visible: fences, highways, rivers, rail tracks. Most are invisible: racial lines, class divides, language zones, codes of belonging. But characters always feel them.

Crossing a boundary isn't just a change in setting—it's a shift in emotional temperature, power dynamic, and story stakes. That movement introduces friction, risk, and sometimes revelation.

A character walking from a luxury high-rise into a public housing complex might feel exposed. Another, crossing from a known cultural enclave into a redlined corridor, might feel unwelcome or surveilled. Someone stepping out of a car and into a crowd, trading private comfort for public scrutiny, might find the city suddenly hostile.

Even for characters used to moving between zones, the movement carries charge. Crossing boundaries often means:

- ▸ Violating a social script
- ▸ Entering a space where the rules shift
- ▸ Becoming visible in a way that wasn't true moments before
- ▸ Carrying part of one world into another—and realizing it doesn't belong

Plot twists can occur at these crossings. So can confessions. So can collapse. These are the places where secrets get told, where reputations

81

fall apart, where truths become undeniable.

Slow the moment. Your character can pause at the line, hesitate before crossing. Notice how the street noise changes. How the language shifts. How the smell in the air reminds them where they are—and who they might not be here.

Where are the lines in your city? Who draws them? Who crosses them? Who pays the price?

Rhythm, Repetition, Disruption

Cities create patterns. So do characters. Repetition in space builds expectation. It gives the illusion of normalcy, stability, and control.

A character walking the same route to work every morning doesn't just know the streets—they feel them. The crack in the sidewalk near the bakery. The crossing guard who never makes eye contact. The smell of grease from the food truck. That route becomes a rhythm—a physical beat that anchors the day.

But when the pattern breaks, the story begins to move.

- They take a different turn
- The bus skips a stop
- Their key doesn't work
- The flower stand is gone
- The usual shortcut is fenced off

These disruptions are not just plot devices. They signal internal or external shifts: grief, avoidance, escalation, growth. Even a small detour—turning left instead of right—can reveal everything the reader needs to know about what's changing inside your character.

Routine signals stasis. Disruption reveals transformation. Detour can expose longing, fear, or refusal. When patterns break, stories turn. That broken rhythm can trigger suspense, emotional rupture, or release.

Readers can feel the rhythm of the city through your character's habits. And they can feel the tension when that rhythm falls apart. That rupture isn't just narrative—it's personal. Because when the city changes, we change with it.

Cityform as Storyform

Cities don't just hold stories. They suggest shapes.

The way a city is designed—its grids, spirals, vertical layers, zones, rupture points—can become the underlying form of a narrative. Plot structure doesn't have to follow a clean arc. It can follow a subway line. A looped bike route. A climb from sewer to ground to rooftop. A journey from surface polish to buried truth.

Linear: The Train Line

Imagine each chapter as a stop: north to south, uptown to downtown. Each one introduces a new atmosphere, a new threat, a new layer of the city—and of the character. The train becomes a spine. But it's also a trap: a one-directional ride where the character sees what's coming but can't get off without consequence. They're in motion, but not in control.

This structure builds momentum and inevitability. As the train moves forward, stakes accumulate. Delays matter. Missed stops matter. Encounters are compressed by proximity, time, and space. By the final stop, the character must make a choice: exit, leap, double back, derail.

This form works literally or metaphorically.

- A noir story that follows a night shift conductor from one neighborhood to the next, descending into darkness.
- A story of emotional unravelling, told through each stop of the morning commute as routine gives way to crisis.
- A thriller where the skipped stop holds the truth—and the climax happens when the train finally goes express.

You can build tension through repetition and variation:

- Each stop can mirror a stage of grief, recovery, or realization.
- Transitions between stops become reflection points— or zones of danger.

- Transfers, delays, and reroutes offer structural surprises that echo the character's shifting trajectory.

This approach is especially useful for stories built around constraint—where characters are trapped in systems (emotional, infrastructural, political) and must either adapt or resist. The train moves, whether they're ready or not.

Loop: The Spiral

Your character returns to the same location—again and again. The apartment door. The corner bodega. The train platform at dusk. But with each return, the emotional context has shifted. What was once ordinary becomes charged, unstable, loaded with weight.

This structure mirrors obsession, grief, repetition compulsion, nostalgia, the refusal to let go. The story doesn't build toward a single explosive climax. Instead, it turns through accumulation—through the emotional gravity that builds with each loop. What matters isn't what happens next, but what changes in the return.

Each pass through the loop might reveal:

- **A new emotional layer** (confusion → denial → rage → numbness)
- **A shift in sensory experience** (a scent that once comforted now disgusts)
- **A change in behavior** (lingering longer, touching the door, walking past)

There are variations:

- A **tightening spiral**—where returns get closer together, more intense, claustrophobic.
- A **widening spiral**—where the return becomes more distant, abstract, or symbolic, like dreaming of a place they no longer visit.
- A **broken spiral**—where the character tries to return but can't. The place is gone, changed, or closed off. That absence becomes the story's pivot.

84

These loops are ideal for:

- ▸ Characters stuck in cycles they can't escape
- ▸ Stories of emotional reckoning without clear resolution
- ▸ Narratives of addiction, grief, memory, or betrayal

The tension lies not in action, but in emotional residue.

Each return is an echo—slightly altered, slightly warped. Eventually, the spiral leads somewhere: collapse, release, change, or refusal.

This structure invites deep interiority. It lets the city become a memory loop, a pressure cooker, a ghost.

Vertical: The Descent or Ascent

Cities are layered—physically, socially, psychologically. A rooftop party has a different tension than a basement interrogation. A pedestrian bridge feels nothing like a tunnel or sewer. These spaces don't just differ in height—they differ in emotional temperature, power dynamics, and narrative potential.

Vertical movement can shape your story's trajectory:

- ▸ Ascend for exposure, power, aspiration, or escape
- ▸ Descend for secrecy, entrapment, collapse, or revelation

Each level brings a new emotional register.

- ▸ A rooftop might expose a character's vulnerability, even as it offers perspective.
- ▸ A stairwell might compress their choices, force confrontation.
- ▸ A descent into a basement could signal either danger or intimacy, depending on how it's staged.
- ▸ An elevator might trap characters between levels— forcing stillness, confession, or collision.

This isn't just set design—it's story logic. A narrative might climb, chapter by chapter, toward higher stakes and sharper visibility, each level shedding comfort or illusion. Or it might fall, peeling back surface layers until the character reaches the raw, buried truth.

Vertical structure doesn't have to move in one direction. It can oscillate:

- A character rises socially or professionally, while descending emotionally.
- A story that rises into clarity, then collapses into chaos.
- A structure where each location pairs a physical level with a moral or psychological turn.

This structure works especially well for stories about:

- Power and hierarchy
- Exposure and concealment
- Transformation under pressure

The city's layers can echo your character's own. Where they are—rooftop or stairwell, basement or bridge—might shape who they're allowed to be, and what they're forced to confront.

Zoning: Emotional Terrain

Urban planners divide space by function. Stories can follow the same logic. Cities are segmented into zones—residential, commercial, industrial—not just to organize land use, but to shape behavior, flow, and visibility. These zones carry emotional and narrative temperature. So do your scenes.

- **Residential zones** = privacy, routine, interiority
- **Commercial zones** = performance, surveillance, transaction
- **Infrastructure/industrial zones** = systems, neglect, labor, decay

Each space sets expectations. A fight in a bedroom lands differently than one in a drugstore. A confession outside a church isn't the same as one whispered in a parking garage. These aren't just settings—they're emotional terrains.

As your character moves between zones, the tone and texture of the story shifts.

- In **residential space**, we expect softness, privacy, vulnerability.
- In **commercial zones**, characters are observed, staged, commodified.
- In **infrastructure**, the stakes shift toward survival, navigation, exposure to systemic forces.

Entire narratives can be structured around zonal movement:

- A story that begins in the intimacy of the home and ends in the impersonal machinery of the city.
- A plot that loops a character through the same zone repeatedly—until it changes, or they do.
- A story where emotional safety is only possible in liminal cracks between zones—rooftops, stairwells, alleyways.

Transitions matter. Moving from a residential space to a commercial one isn't just physical—it's emotional. Boundaries reveal friction: shame, power shifts, fear of exposure.

Those crossings can shape how your characters behave, what they say, and what they hold back. Pressure can rise through spatial logic. Geography can surface what emotion tries to hide.

Gentrification as Arc

Cities change. Stories can too.

Begin in a polished, redeveloped space—clean lines, branded signage, curated aesthetic. A place that looks like safety but feels like performance. Then move deeper. Past the new coffee shop. Past the commissioned mural. Into the parts of the city still in flux—or already erased.

Gentrification isn't just backdrop. It's narrative structure.

- **Act I: Surface Safety.** A world that seems stable, desirable, controlled. The character accepts this version of the city—or benefits from it. There's comfort in the

87

clean façade, but also disconnection. Someone is missing. Something feels off.

- ▸ **Act II: Cracks in the Image.** Small ruptures appear. A neighbor is evicted. A beloved store disappears. A protest flickers past. The character begins to notice who gets to stay—and who disappears. Tension builds between appearances and impact. What once seemed like progress now feels like erasure.
- ▸ **Act III: Exposure and Resistance.** The character moves into contested space. A homecoming, a confrontation, a rupture. Maybe they reclaim something. Maybe they lose something. Maybe they realize they were part of the problem. The city's layers are no longer hidden—and neither are theirs.

This arc resonates especially with stories of:

- ▸ **Return** (to a city, a home, a self)
- ▸ **Disillusionment** (with power, identity, privilege)
- ▸ **Belonging and erasure** (who gets written into the city and who gets pushed out)
- ▸ **Awakening** (when comfort cracks and complicity is revealed)

The city's transformation can echo the character's own. As the surface peels back, truth emerges. As neighborhoods shift, so do allegiances, values, and memory. Sometimes the journey is from outsider to insider. Other times, from insider to exile.

Gentrification, like story, is layered: aesthetic, economic, emotional. Its arc can structure revelation, tension, and return.

The Corridor Story

Some cities funnel people through narrow paths: alleys, viaducts, underpasses—corridors that compress the body and narrow the options. These aren't just physical structures—they're metaphors for pressure, inevitability, ritual, or entrapment.

A corridor story doesn't branch. It tunnels. There are no side doors, no alternate endings. The only way out is through.

This structure works especially well for stories of:

- **Trauma**—where the path must be walked to reach reckoning
- **Obsession or ritual**—where every step is preordained, repeated, unavoidable
- **Systems of power**—where prisons, bureaucracies, institutions resist deviation

Each scene becomes a door—opened reluctantly, or forced open—that reveals something deeper:

- A risk taken
- A memory faced
- A truth confronted

This corridor form can be used literally or metaphorically:

- A character physically moves through a long hallway, tunnel, or corridor-like neighborhood (rail lines, housing blocks, industrial zones)
- A character progresses through a rigid timeline or ritual, unable to skip steps or break form
- A story where deviation is impossible and resistance must happen inside the structure, not beyond it

This form builds narrative claustrophobia. The walls don't just narrow space—they narrow choice. As the story progresses, the corridor tightens—shorter chapters, fewer options, sharper consequences. Momentum builds not from expansion, but from compression.

The Fragmented Grid

Not all cities follow a plan. Some were redlined, then rezoned. Some were built in layers—colonial atop Indigenous, financial atop residential. Some were abandoned in pieces. A fragmented city creates a fragmented story. This is the logic of rupture—a narrative shaped by what's missing.

Instead of clean arcs or continuous movement, the story skips, loops, hesitates. Locations are revisited but altered. Chapters end mid-thought. A detail appears, then vanishes. A question is asked but never answered. The reader assembles meaning the way a pedestrian navigates a half-erased map.

This form mirrors:

- **Trauma**—where memory is partial, nonlinear, or blocked
- **Diaspora**—where belonging is scattered, inherited, or lost
- **Dislocation**—where characters can't fully anchor in space or self
- **Urban erasure**—where neighborhoods are erased, renamed, or fenced off

This structure is less concerned with plot coherence and more with plot atmosphere.

- The gaps matter.
- The silences are where meaning lives.
- The structure itself becomes a story of survival.

You might:

- Skip whole locations or time periods, then allude to them later through sensory recall
- Use recurring places that shift slightly each time—displaced in space or tone
- Fragment your syntax or formatting to mirror psychic fracture
- Include absences as narrative beats: the person who isn't there, the demolished place, the map with the street scratched out

Emotional resonance doesn't come from what happens next—but from what didn't happen, what couldn't, or what had to be left behind. The structure invites the reader to work—to hold uncertainty, to make meaning from debris. It's a form to consider when your story remembers what others forgot.

The Sprawl Story

Some cities grow outward, not upward. With no center. No clear boundary. Just arterial roads, subdivisions, strip malls, off-ramps. Endless beige.

In a sprawl story, your character doesn't move toward a goal. They move across a landscape that refuses focus. There's no anchor. No terminal point. Just more of the same. The story becomes about drift, exhaustion, dislocation, repetition. Maybe they keep driving. Maybe they walk through identical intersections, chasing a past that won't stay still.

This is a story of decentralization. The anti-structure. A plot that resists climactic moments and instead builds a low, humming unease.

Think of it like a big-box parking lot at dusk. Flat. Wide. Lonely. That can be structure, too.

This form works well for stories about:

  ‣ **Alienation in late capitalism**—chasing meaning in a landscape built for consumption, not connection
  ‣ **Emotional dissociation**—where characters move without clear cause or direction
  ‣ **Grief or loss**—where resolution never arrives—only accumulation

Narrative tools might include:

  ‣ Scenes that begin to repeat—but not quite identically
  ‣ Encounters that feel interchangeable, even when they matter
  ‣ Settings that blur: another fast-food counter, another chain pharmacy, another empty road
  ‣ An ending that fades rather than resolves

Characters in sprawl stories may:

  ‣ **Be adrift**—aware they're lost but unsure how to stop

- **Be complicit**—numbing themselves through movement and sameness
- **Be in pursuit**—chasing something (or someone) that no longer exists

This structure is atmospheric. It works through saturation, not escalation. It asks the reader to sit with discomfort, disorientation, flatness—to feel what it's like to move through a world with no topography of meaning.

The city's shape can guide your story's form. Not all stories climb. Some spiral. Some fracture. Some follow the train. But some flatten. Some blur. Some drift. And sometimes, the sprawl is the point.

In Summary

Cities aren't just *where* stories happen. They shape *how* stories happen. They offer:

- A logic of movement
- A scaffolding of tension
- A language of boundary and breach

Plot can emerge from place. Conflict can be structured by setting. Geography can unsettle expectation. When your character moves through the city, readers should feel every step, every stop, every refusal. A city isn't just a backdrop. It's a blueprint. A pressure system. A map of conflict and constraint.

Plot lives in the map—if you know how to read it.

Exercise 1: Plot as Map

Prompt: Draw your city—real or imagined. Mark major scenes. Draw movement between them as if they were train stops or bus lines.

Questions to explore:

- Is this motion linear? Circular? Erratic?
- Where do things slow down—or stall completely?
- Where is the climax, and why does it happen *there*?
- What spaces are avoided—and what does that reveal?

Sample Answer

The story begins in Uptown, where the protagonist works the night shift at a 24-hour diner. Most scenes unfold along the Red Line: a confrontation at Belmont, a breakdown at Harrison, a final decision at 95th/Dan Ryan. The map is linear but uneven—the southbound trip intensifies with each stop. The climax happens at a transfer point: Roosevelt, where the protagonist must choose whether to stay on the train or change direction. The West Side is completely absent—not because it doesn't matter, but because the character refuses to go where their grief lives.

Exercise 2: Rewrite in Space

Prompt: Take one scene—a confrontation, a confession, a kiss. Rewrite it in two different city settings:

- **A tight space** (elevator, stairwell, bathroom)
- **A wide-open space** (plaza, festival, parking lot)

Sample Answer

Tight Space—Apartment Stairwell

In the narrow stairwell between the third and fourth floor, the confrontation feels compressed. The air is stale. One fluorescent bulb flickers overhead. Their voices drop—harsher in whisper, more intimate in proximity. No one can storm off. Every word feels boxed in, close-range, dangerous. The tension is trapped with them.

Wide-Open Space—Daley Plaza

In the middle of Daley Plaza during lunch rush, the same confrontation becomes spectacle. Strangers glance, then look away. A food truck speaker blasts bachata in the background. The dialogue is sharper, meaner, public. What was intimate becomes exposed. The city doesn't offer cover—only witnesses.

Same scene. Different city pressure.

Exercise 3: Follow the Boundary

Prompt: Write a scene where your character must cross a visible or invisible boundary—geographic, social, cultural. Slow the crossing. Focus on the textures of change: shifts in language, surveillance, noise, signage, emotion.

Sample Answer

A teenager from Jefferson Park takes the Blue Line to Pilsen to find someone who might know what happened to his older brother. He switches trains at Clark/Lake. The crowd changes. By the time he's on the Pink Line, the signs are bilingual, the rhythm of the car different. As he walks down 18th Street, he notices the murals first—faces he doesn't recognize but that seem to be watching him. There's a street vendor with tamales. A church letting out. He pulls his hoodie up. He doesn't know if he's trespassing or arriving. He doesn't speak the language. But he walks anyway.

7

When the City Remembers

Walk through any city and you'll feel it: the weight of what came before. Sometimes it's overt—a bronze plaque marking where a resistance met the pavement, a statue quietly removed, a street renamed. Other times it's more atmospheric: the cracked mosaic floor in a new bar that still smells faintly of fryer grease from its former life, or the way an alley seems to remember the people who once hid there.

Cities aren't just spatial—they're temporal. They hold time the way old houses hold scent: deep in the floorboards, long after the people are gone. You may not see the past clearly, but it presses through—in texture, in rhythm, in absence. When you write cities, the work isn't just to map the present, it's to write the past as pressure: lingering, shaping, sometimes erupting through the seams of the everyday.

City memory is more than historical detail. It's narrative tension. What has been forgotten, and by whom? What lingers unspoken in architecture, in infrastructure, in public space? Whose stories were paved over—and what still seeps up through the cracks? Fiction can gain emotional resonance when it acknowledges that no city is ever in a single time zone. Cities are time-collisions. Their ruins, renovations, rituals, and rhythms are in constant conversation. Your characters walk through layers.

If Chapters 1–5 asked you to treat cities as characters—with temperament, power, constraint, narrative rhythm, and voice—then this chapter invites you to give those characters memory. Because cities don't forget—and when fiction remembers, it deepens.

City memory can take many forms:

- The emotional residue of a demolished building.
- A generational trauma mapped onto a street grid.
- The tension between official history and lived experience.
- The shadow of a protest painted over, but still visible in cracks and soot.
- A name carved into a bus shelter no one claims, but no one erases.
- The detour that's become permanent because no one can quite bear to return.
- A rusted chain-link fence that outlasts four renovations—and a memory of who it was meant to keep out.

You don't need to write historical fiction to write historically. Contemporary stories set in cities live in rebranded neighborhoods, in renamed streets, in silenced blocks that still echo with their former lives. The deeper a city's memory, the more emotionally resonant a story can become. Because what's remembered—and what isn't—is never neutral. Memory is political. Memory is plot. Memory is character.

This chapter will show you how to:

- Use time as atmosphere and mood
- Embed historical depth in infrastructure and detail
- Explore urban arcs and generational change
- Layer personal memory over collective memory
- Reveal how grief and loss imprint themselves onto the built environment
- Write fiction that feels rooted, haunted, resonant, alive

Cities, like people, are never just who they are—they are who they've been. Fiction that reflects that complexity often carries more emotional weight.

The Palimpsest City

A palimpsest is a manuscript that's been scraped clean and written over—but the original text never fully disappears. It lingers in ghosted ink, warped fibers, faded strokes. Cities are architectural palimpsests: overwritten again and again by waves of development, demolition, reinvention, and forgetting.

Every new building, every renamed street, every polished redevelopment project is laid on top of what came before. And what came before rarely stays quiet. In stories set in cities, acknowledging that buried past isn't just a gesture toward realism—it's a way to tap into deeper narrative tension.

It may help to think of your city as a text with layers: some legible, others half-erased. What's still visible? What's been scraped away—and by whom? Who gets to write over the past, and who gets written over?

Where the Past Presses Through: Two Chicago Palimpsests

Fulton Market

The West Loop's Fulton Market district today gleams with glass facades, rooftop bars, and Michelin-starred restaurants. But it was once a dense hub of meatpacking and food distribution: a web of loading docks, cold storage warehouses, and small-scale slaughterhouses that operated in tandem with the larger Union Stockyards to the south.

If you look closely, traces remain: a rusting hook on a brick façade, a fading *Poultry & Eggs* sign above a boutique, a weathered steel track running overhead from a defunct meat hoist. The industry's scale here was smaller than the stockyards of Back of the Yards—but it shaped the district's working-class identity for decades.

The bodies are gone. The smell is gone. But the bones remain.

In Back of the Yards, the echoes are more skeletal—empty lots where the massive Yards once sprawled, a mural here or there, a street named "Exchange." The neighborhood bears the scars of deindustrialization more visibly than the West Loop's polished surfaces. But both places are palimpsests—just with different layers exposed, or reburied.

Look past what a place is. You might hear what it used to be.

A character might walk down Lake Street and wonder why the sidewalk glints with embedded metal—leftover from a long-forgotten rail spur used for meat deliveries. They might catch their sleeve on a jagged bracket jutting from the brick—once part of a pulley system used to hoist carcasses overhead. Those stories are gone now. But the metal remains. The sidewalk still glints. And what's buried still shapes what happens. A character might feel watched in a luxury condo—not by ghosts, but by the history they paved over.

These aren't Easter eggs for urban historians. They're tools for emotional layering. When a character senses the city's layers—even unconsciously—fiction can gain a second register. A past that presses up through the floorboards.

Printers Row

Head south from the Loop and you'll enter Printers Row—a neighborhood where the past hasn't been erased so much as carved in stone. Between the 1880s and the 1950s, more than forty buildings lined Dearborn Street in the shadow of Dearborn Station, firmly establishing this as Chicago's hub of printing and publishing. The station opened in 1885 and handled thousands of workers and freight cars daily, bringing in skilled labor and sending out printed material across the Midwest.

Walk the blocks between Ida B. Wells and Polk, and you'll see the bones of that era: fortress-like buildings with narrow windows and massive brick façades, built to resist fires from volatile presses. The Donohue Building, opened in 1883, still bears its name in Romanesque stone—once home to dime-novel and textbook production. The Franklin Building, with its colorful terracotta frieze, depicts binders and printers, even a scroll announcing the "First Impression"—a carved tribute to Gutenberg's legacy.

You don't need a historian to read the history here. The buildings tell their own stories.

Even today, the corridors hold traces of what came before. Ceilings soar high, once designed to vent press-heat. Windows run long and narrow to manage fire risk. And at the corner of Federal and Harrison, a hulking printing press stands on display—public art that isn't decoration. It's testimony.

Meanwhile, Dearborn Station looms just a stone's throw south. Its clock tower still marks time, even though passenger service ended in 1971. The yards once filled with freight cars, postal wagons, and presses; now they're Dearborn Park. Though revitalized into offices and retail, the station carries emotional freight—often cited as the gateway for immigrant workers and the spark for Printers Row's rise.

In fiction, this layered space offers rich narrative currency.

- A character might awake in a Donohue loft to the imagined rumble of a train pulling out of Dearborn Station in the night.
- A digital archivist might pass the printing press on Federal, feeling a tug of memory for an industry that shaped the city.
- A scene at the station's clock tower might mark a turning point—arrival, departure, longing—echoing the hundreds who passed through on their way to work and life in Chicago.

When your characters inhabit Printers Row, they walk through multiple eras: the age of transit, the golden era of printing, the decline of both press and rail, and the rise of the loft renaissance. Each building, each artifact, carries a sedimented story—ready for you to unearth.

Characters might move through this neighborhood not as tourists, but as people haunted by what the buildings still hold: labor, noise, paper, ambition, loss. Your fiction can do what cities do: hold history in plain sight, and pretend it's invisible. In a city layered with memory, your characters aren't just moving through streets—they're moving through residues of ambition, grief, and something left unresolved. Their footsteps can echo with what was once there.

Writing Time as Mood

Cities carry mood—and mood often emerges not from what a city is, but from what time it thinks it's in.

Time in cities isn't linear. It's atmospheric. It gathers in pockets and eddies. Some neighborhoods feel paused in the 1950s, others feel pulled ten years into a techy, antiseptic future. A city's mood often emerges from this uneven layering—from a tension between the eras still visible, the ones selectively glorified, and the ones purposefully erased.

As a writer, ask yourself:

- What decade does this city think it's in?
- What part of its past is it obsessed with?
- What era is it trying to erase?
- What event hangs in the air, unspoken but felt?

These questions aren't just for setting description—they're emotional diagnostics. A city stuck in nostalgia might produce characters who resist change, cling to loss, or retreat into memory. A city charging toward reinvention might accelerate your plot but may flatten your protagonist—unless you build in resistance, friction, or cultural whiplash.

Some cities wear history like a scar. Detroit, Havana, Naples—places where the past isn't neatly memorialized but exposed, unglossed, alive. Their architecture is cracked, their timelines visible. The mood they generate defies the label of "ruin porn"—it's endurance. It's trauma. It's persistence.

Other cities—Shenzhen, Dubai, parts of Atlanta—stage futurity. They perform speed, erasure, ambition. Construction cranes outnumber playgrounds. Memory is not invited. These cities feel breathless, abstract, always arriving but never *arriving*. The mood is forward-pitched, often anxious.

Chicago splits the difference. It's a city that selectively mythologizes its past—bootlegging, jazz, machine politics—while quietly bulldozing large portions of it. You can take a gangster tour in River North, sipping a themed cocktail in a fake speakeasy. But a mile away are the remnants of neighborhoods destroyed by redlining, freeway construction, or Chicago Housing Authority demolition—barely acknowledged. Chicago freezes certain moments in amber—noir murals, flapper bar kitsch—while others are quietly paved over. That disjointed temporal awareness creates a powerful, sometimes melancholic mood.

And that mood is charged. It produces friction—between neighborhoods, between generations, between the official story and the lived one.

Writing the Past Shapes the Present

You don't need to set a story in the past to evoke the past. You can write contemporary fiction that feels like history is present—pressing against your characters, reshaping their choices, suffusing the air.

Consider:

▸ A story about economic precarity might unfold in a gentrifying district where glossy new signage sits on cracked brick, and the mural of a labor organizer is slowly fading under scaffolding.

▸ A story about cultural resistance might be set in a city that's trying hard to forget the last time its youth rebelled—where the police station has been renovated, but the trauma it holds remains unspoken.

▸ A romance might bloom in a neighborhood that feels suspended in another decade—soft lighting, old signage, a slowed-down tempo that makes the characters feel like they've slipped out of time.

▸ A grief story might unfold in a place caught in stasis—where nothing has been built in years, and the ghosts linger openly.

The emotional weather of your fiction is shaped by time—not clock time, but city time: how a place holds memory, loss, ambition, denial. These aren't backdrops. They're battlegrounds of memory. And memory, in fiction, is mood.

Memory in the Infrastructure

Urban space tells stories even when no one is speaking. Architecture leaks memory. Infrastructure holds grief. Public space mutters its past beneath your characters' feet.

The city doesn't need to tell you what happened. It shows you—

101

in the slant of a wall, the shape of a street corner, the ghost outlines on brick where signage once hung. History embeds itself in material—and material doesn't forget.

A rusting metal sign for a long-shuttered diner still juts from a building now occupied by a vape shop. The paint is chipped, the phone number obsolete, but the font—bold, friendly, almost innocent—whispers of a different era. It doesn't need to be explained. Just let a character look up and feel something.

Or maybe a former public housing complex has been razed, replaced by a sleek new retail development with parking underneath. Official signs no longer name the complex, but people still say, "Get off at Cabrini."

A character might pause at an intersection where the bricks are just slightly mismatched—redder in tone, slightly newer in shape. They might not know that a protest once erupted here, that a police cruiser was set on fire, that those bricks were replaced quietly and quickly. But the city remembers. And if you write that detail—if you let your character feel the irregularity underfoot—then your fiction remembers too.

These traces of memory aren't always marked by plaques or preserved in museums. They linger in infrastructure, language, and everyday surfaces. Writers can learn to tune into them. In Chicago, memory leaks through the very roads. Here are a few ways it shows up:

- Street signs in Pilsen remain in both English and Spanish, even as the neighborhood gentrifies.
- A sculpted terra cotta arch from the Chicago Stock Exchange building now stands outside the Art Institute—collected after the original was demolished.
- Bronze markers on the sidewalk downtown trace the route of the Great Chicago Fire.
- A concrete foundation near the lakefront outlines the ghost of a demolished hospital.
- Real estate listings rename neighborhoods as "West Bucktown" or "Logan East," but longtime residents resist those terms—mapping their own memories over the city grid.

These aren't just remnants. They're narrative pressure points—fragments that keep the past vibrating just beneath the present.

The Harold Washington Library Center downtown looms with postmodern grandeur, all red granite and green roof filigree. It's named for Chicago's first Black mayor—a visionary figure whose election marked a seismic shift in the city's racial and political history. But how many people walk past it without remembering who Harold Washington was, what he stood for, how he died in office, what that loss meant? The memory is in the name. But only if you look.

On the South Side, abandoned churches stand in ruin. Until its recent landmark grant, Pilgrim Baptist in Bronzeville remained a gutted shell after a fire left only its exterior walls standing. In Auburn Gresham, the Little Flower Church has sat vacant for years, its stained-glass windows shattered or missing, its interior decayed. Many closed under the weight of disinvestment rather than demolition, leaving architecture that once housed song and sanctuary to quietly collapse. These places remain—not honored, but present—with histories built into broken bricks and fading glass.

These are not tourist sites. There are no plaques. But they are dense with narrative potential.

Some moments don't need explanation. Memory can settle into the scenery. A pause says enough. So can silence. A character doesn't need to know what happened in a particular space for that space to feel charged. Sometimes the city remembers for them—bearing the weight of sorrow, survival, and things left unresolved.

Stillness can carry some of the weight. Infrastructure is not neutral. It is history you can touch—or trip over. Fiction can notice what the city holds, what it hides, and what it cannot help but reveal.

Ghosts and Echoes

Sometimes time isn't just a mood—it manifests. The past doesn't stay buried. It erupts. It flickers. It knocks once and waits for your character to notice.

A character flinches at a street name. A building gives them vertigo. A piece of graffiti—a name, a date, a fragment of an old chant—

shakes something loose. These aren't plot points. They're psychic ruptures. The past insisting on being felt.

This isn't necessarily surreal or uncanny—though it might feel that way. It's emotional realism. Cities are full of sites where memory becomes physical. Sometimes it's a sharp pang. Sometimes it's just a shift in temperature, an unsettled breath. Either way, the city is speaking— or echoing something your character thought they'd forgotten.

You don't have to spell it out. Feeling can intrude. It colors the moment. It slips through sensation and suddenly the past is in the room. Consider:

- A queer teenager finds shelter in a dive bar downtown. The music is good, the crowd is soft. But when sirens pass outside, they flinch—not because they did anything wrong, but because decades ago, this bar was routinely raided, its patrons arrested and outed. That history isn't in the décor. It's in the atmosphere.

- A father crosses a bridge on the South Branch of the river. Midway across, he stops. It's not conscious at first. Then he remembers: a friend jumped from this spot during the 1995 heatwave, when the city failed to warn or protect. He doesn't say it aloud. But it hits— and he doesn't keep walking.

- A character stares up at a mirrored office tower. From the outside, it's all angles and reflection. But twenty years ago, it was a women's shelter. She stayed there once, briefly. Now it's glass and marketing copy. Her reflection stares back at her, older. The memory comes fast—the cold floor, the fluorescent light, the kindness of a stranger. She's not sad. She's not angry. She's just there again.

Ghosts don't need to be literal. Cities are haunted by erasure, by absence, by memory that clings to corners and stairwells. Sometimes it's personal. Sometimes it's collective. Sometimes your character doesn't even know the story—but they feel the weight of it.

Sometimes the ghost is narrative: a repeated image, a line someone mutters that shouldn't mean anything—but does. A smell that arrives on a hot day and brings a character back thirty years without warning.

Time doesn't always stay in the background. It ruptures the surface of the narrative. The past barges in, uninvited. Fiction often deepens when memory intrudes—when your character is just trying to live in the now, but the city won't let them forget.

The City's Arc Over Time

Cities are not static. They don't just exist—they transform. And those transformations, like any good narrative arc, come with tension, conflict, and consequence.

Some cities rise, flush with new capital, new architecture, new names on the skyline. Others fall, hollowed out by disinvestment, depopulation, decay. Some attempt to rebrand—layering fresh language, fresh paint, fresh mythologies over deep wounds. The city's arc is never smooth. It's turbulent, lurching, often tragic. And it rarely benefits everyone.

Writers can trace that arc—or disrupt it. The work isn't just noticing what the city looks like, but who it's becoming. And at whose expense. Ask yourself:

- Is your city rising? Are cranes everywhere, tech companies moving in, neighborhoods renamed with fake district branding? Does the city feel like it's hurtling toward something—or running from something?
- Is your city falling? Are the roads cratered, the schools closing, the lights dimming? Are people leaving, not arriving?
- Is your city rebranding? Are tourism campaigns smoothing over old scars? Are the unhoused being swept before conventions? Are plaques going up even as stories are coming down?

These arcs aren't just aesthetic or economic. They're emotional. They're political. And they create real narrative stakes.

Consider Chicago: The Loop has transformed more than once in

105

a single generation—once a bustling center of finance and department stores, it emptied after dark; gentrified into the home of high-rise condos and rooftop bars; was silenced by COVID; and is now reimagining itself again, caught between commercial vacancies and lifestyle reinvention. That churn isn't just demographic—it's psychological. It breeds restlessness, anxiety, and a strange form of amnesia.

In Pilsen, vibrant murals preserve Mexican identity, protest displacement, and mourn disappearance. Yet parts of the Lower West Side are being marketed under the community name "Heart of Chicago," a label that overlooks Pilsen's working-class and immigrant roots. That's not just rebranding—it's narrative warfare. And fiction can lean into that tension: between the story the neighborhood tells and the one being sold.

The South Side has long suffered from underinvestment, but parts of Bronzeville are blooming again—not through mass development, but through small-scale revival: community gardens, bookstores, block parties, oral history projects. These are signs of resurgence. They're signs of resistance—of a city refusing to be defined by its lowest moment.

Urban arcs are rarely fair. So the questions shift:

- Who survives this transformation?
- Who resists it?
- Who profits from the forgetting?
- Who carries the memory forward?

Because forgetting is often the goal. A new restaurant opens where a union hall used to be. A sleek apartment tower rises where a community kitchen once stood. And if no one tells the story, if no one remembers, then the city's arc appears smooth. Unbroken. But fiction can fracture that illusion.

Cities deserve narrative arcs—not just timelines, but trajectories. They rise and fall. They hurt and recover. And their transformation should collide with your characters'. Maybe they're shaped by it. Maybe they're crushed by it. Maybe they fight back. But no one moves through a city frozen in time.

And fiction shouldn't either.

In Summary

Time doesn't move evenly through a city. It lingers. It loops. It leaks. It resurfaces. In fiction, time isn't just a backdrop—it's a force. It shapes atmosphere, animates infrastructure, ruptures plot, and haunts character. Cities are layered:

- Architecturally
- Emotionally
- Politically
- Narratively

Those layers don't always announce themselves. But they shape how a city is felt—and how a story unfolds. Memory can live in detail, in tension, in absence. Not just in exposition, but in texture and tone. Time might appear as:

- A crack in the pavement
- A smell on a summer street
- A skyline that no longer matches the map
- A name said with longing—or not said at all

In fiction, memory can be structure. And cities don't forget. The next chapter explores how time doesn't just haunt the city—it organizes it: patterns, pulses, pace. Plot and transformation, too, are spatial.

Exercise 1: The Layered Location

Prompt: Choose a location in your novel—or invent one. Describe it from three different points in time:

- 30 years ago
- 10 years ago
- Today

Then write a fourth paragraph set in the present, where your protagonist walks through the space. How do those layers linger? What changes do they notice—or fail to notice? Use this moment to shift tone, build tension, or uncover something quietly buried in the character.

Sample Answer (Chicago: Maxwell Street Market)

30 years ago: Maxwell Street still buzzed with vendors hawking tube socks, bootleg cassettes, tacos, and tools. A man plays blues on a corner while someone else grills Polish sausages in a metal drum cut lengthwise. The air smells like charcoal and diesel—an electric blues backdrop to a bustling market.

10 years ago: The market has been pushed east—to Canal, then to Desplaines. Most old-school vendors are gone. A few food stalls remain, but everything feels temporary, and the street musicians have moved on.

Today: Now it's a curated, city-backed farmers' market, returned to Maxwell and Halsted. You'll find artisan bread, kombucha, clean sidewalks, piped-in blues music, and plaques commemorating the market's history—but few actual musicians.

Layered moment: Your character walks the street, sipping coffee, unsure why they feel hollow. They step over a rust stain, glance at a plaque honoring Muddy Waters—and for a moment they think they hear a guitar riff echoing from the past, though no one's playing now.

Exercise 2: Write the Echo

Prompt: Think of a place in your city where something significant happened—personally, politically, culturally—even if your character doesn't know the story. Write a scene where the character passes through that space and feels... something. Unease. Wonder. Grief. A strange sense of recognition. Then, slowly or suddenly, let memory surface—whether personal, historical, or imagined. Then flip the perspective. What would the city say about that place, if it could remember?

Sample Answer (Chicago: Bronzeville)

Your character is new to Chicago. They get off the Red Line at 35th-Bronzeville-IIT, drawn in by a mural. As they walk past an old hardware store, they feel a strange quiet. Later, they learn that block used to house the Sunset Café—a legendary jazz club where Louis Armstrong played, where Nat King Cole got his start. It closed decades ago, but the bones are still there.

They return the next day. This time, they stop. And listen. Nothing but traffic. But still—something lingers.

If the block could speak, it might hum. A horn riff left behind in the mortar. A heel scuff in rhythm under the sidewalk dust. It remembers the heat, the suits, the sound that poured through its windows and rose into the night. It remembers what joy sounded like—before the silence settled in.

Exercise 3: Chart the City's Arc

Prompt: Cities evolve—and not always evenly. Names shift. Borders blur. Memory gets overwritten. But not everyone experiences that change the same way. In this exercise, you'll trace your city's transformation and use it to generate conflict, memory, or character perspective.

Step 1: Sketch the Arc

Choose a neighborhood and trace its transformation in three stages:

Then → Disruption → Now

Sample Answer

Then: A working-class Black neighborhood with vibrant community institutions—churches, corner stores, barbershops, basketball courts, and block parties. Neighbors knew each other. Kids walked to school. Block clubs kept things clean. The ice cream truck came at the same time every summer afternoon.

Disruption: Factories closed. The city withdrew investment. Vacant lots spread. Schools and clinics shut down. Gun violence rose, and headlines replaced history. People who stayed made do, held on, and took care of each other—but the city stopped showing up.

109

Now: Developers move in, branding the area as "up-and-coming." New builds rise where bungalows stood. Cafés replace the storefront churches. Yoga studios, wine bars, and dog groomers follow. Longtime residents are priced out or bought out. The city calls it progress. But it doesn't feel like progress to everyone.

Step 2: Add a Character

Pick a point of view:

- A lifelong resident who remembers what was lost
- A newcomer who only knows the "now" version
- Someone who left and returned
- Someone working for the city, tasked with erasing or preserving that memory

Try writing from that character's perspective. How do they carry the arc? What's visible to them—and what isn't?

Sample Answer

Character paragraph: Troy adjusts the city-issued badge clipped to his chest as he steps out of the municipal SUV. The sidewalk gleams— fresh pavers, solar lights, a painted bike lane no one in his old crew would've dared ride. Across the street, the lot yawns empty where Greater Union Missionary Baptist used to stand before the fire. He remembers Easter suits stiff with starch, tambourines shaking the floorboards, the warmth of food, hair grease, cologne, and song in the air. Now there's a *Coming Soon* sign: 34-unit luxury condos with quartz countertops and "urban views." He nods at the site supervisor, makes the inspection notes, says nothing. That's the job. But when he drives off, he doesn't take the highway. He cuts through his old block—just to see what's left. Just to prove to himself it was real.

8

When the City Won't Sit Still

In the last chapter, we explored how cities carry time—how they remember, forget, haunt, and echo. But memory isn't the whole story. Cities don't just hold the past. They also lurch into the future, often violently, often unevenly. They change.

Not just structurally. Not just demographically. Cities change in mood, in pace, in what they make possible. And when a city changes—or refuses to—fiction gains weight, movement, and risk.

Writers often understand that characters need arcs—to grow, unravel, evolve. But we don't always apply that same logic to setting. A city, like a character, can transform. It can strain against itself—or the people who live in it. It can react.

Cities are never finished. They're always in motion—always becoming, or refusing to.

The City in Motion

Even if your story spans a single day, the city isn't still. It's shifting constantly—above ground and below it. The weather changes, scaffolding goes up, a shop closes without notice. Trash accumulates in one block and gets cleared in another. An eviction notice gets taped to a door. The mood of the street tilts, just slightly, and something unspoken shifts in your character's chest.

Cities are never frozen—not in time, not in space, not in feeling. They change in at least three key ways:

- ▸ **Physically**: Cranes appear. Sidewalks crack. A childhood diner becomes a gym with floor-to-ceiling windows. A public transit line is rerouted, and now an entire neighborhood feels more distant. A beloved bookstore is boarded up overnight—not with ceremony, but with plywood.

- ▸ **Socially**: Policy shifts. A protest swells at city hall. Rent spikes in a district and new residents arrive with different rhythms, different languages, different needs. Policing increases in one area and relaxes in another. The feeling of who belongs where—and when—begins to wobble.

- ▸ **Emotionally**: What your protagonist once feared, they now miss. A block that was once busy now feels hollow. Or perhaps a quiet park becomes the only place they feel real. Even if the layout doesn't change, the space's meaning does—and that change is emotional, not architectural.

These layers of transformation aren't just background. They can shape texture, tension, and tone. They influence how your characters move through the world—and how the world moves through them.

A love story hits differently in a city recovering from collapse—still shaky, still scarred, but blooming in the cracks. A story of rage lands differently in a city where the murals are being painted over, where the protest chants have faded from the walls but not the memory. A coming-of-age story gains urgency in a city where childhood landmarks are vanishing one by one—not due to trauma, but due to unchecked reinvention. A grief story deepens in a city that's been scrubbed too clean—where the places that once held memory have been glassed over, renamed, or erased, leaving only the ache of what used to anchor you.

And sometimes the change is invisible but unmistakable. A friend is no longer at their usual stoop. A block feels louder than it used to.

The corner store's gate is down, and no one says why. The train doesn't stop like it used to—but when it passes, the windows glow with colors you don't remember.

You don't need to write an epic to write a city that moves. Even in a short story set over two hours, allow something to shift—a skyline dimming behind storm clouds, a scent, a voice on the street, a rule. Cities breathe under your scenes. That breath should register.

These questions can shape how transformation enters your story—quietly or explosively, personally or politically:

- What is your city becoming—structurally, socially, spiritually?
- What's being lost—and who notices?
- Who is the change for—and who's paying the cost?
- What kind of memory does the city keep—and what does it let fade?
- Where does change stall—and who is left waiting?

When a city moves, it's never neutral. And neither is the narrative shaped by its friction, flow, or refusal.

Parallel or Collision: City and Character in Motion

In fiction, we talk a lot about conflict—internal versus external, character versus character, person versus world. But one of the most potent forms of narrative tension comes from the relationship between the city's arc and the character's arc. Do they move together? Or tear away from each other?

Like any strong secondary character, the city can either echo the protagonist's evolution or resist it. It can serve as a mirror, amplifying what's already in motion, or as a foil, challenging every step forward.

When the trajectories align, the story often feels fated—loss mirrored by ruin, joy by rebirth. But when they diverge, the dissonance creates friction. A character may begin to feel out of sync with the world around them, unmoored or newly alert. That dissonance isn't just thematic—it can drive action, alter perception, or force a reckoning. Whether the city moves with or against the character, the result is a charged atmosphere that makes even ordinary moments hum with tension.

When the city mirrors the character

Sometimes, a protagonist and their city are in sync—both collapsing, or both clawing toward something new. This alignment creates a kind of narrative amplification: everything reverberates louder.

A protagonist is unraveling after a loss—and the city around them is coming apart: storefronts shuttering, trash piling up, services failing. Their personal grief is mirrored in cracked sidewalks and flickering streetlights.

A character on the cusp of healing finds themselves in a city slowly blooming back to life—the park finally reopens, the food trucks return to the plaza, a mural gets painted over a boarded-up window.

In these cases, the city becomes a kind of external nervous system: what's happening inside the character is written across the landscape.

This mirroring doesn't just reinforce mood—it can create the sensation that the city itself is responding, almost empathetically, to the character's inner state. Whether that feeling is real, imagined, or symbolic doesn't matter; what matters is the emotional atmosphere it creates. In these moments, the boundary between self and environment blurs. The city begins to collaborate in the character's transformation, offering signals, rhythms, or echoes that feel intimate—even if no one else notices them.

> *Example:* A woman recovering from an abusive relationship walks through a neighborhood that once felt closed and gray. But now she sees kids playing soccer again on the corner lot, and a street musician she hasn't heard in years is back on his milk crate. It's not all better. But something is waking up—outside and in.

When the city counters the character

Other times, the city and character move in opposite directions. That dissonance creates pressure, disorientation, emotional complexity.

The protagonist is growing, softening, daring to open—but the city is hardening: police presence increases, neighbors stop waving, a friend gets evicted.

A character is stuck in grief or fear, unable to move—and the city moves without them: beloved places close, old rituals vanish, the sounds of the block change.

This contradiction can be heartbreaking. Or enraging. Or galvanizing. Either way, it sharpens the emotional terrain.

When the city moves against the character, it can feel like betrayal. A moment of personal growth or clarity is met not with support, but with indifference—or worse, erasure. This tension can provoke a crisis: is the character resilient enough to withstand the city's pushback, or will they retreat? Sometimes the pressure forces action. Other times, it deepens isolation. But even in silence, this mismatch creates a charged atmosphere where every gesture—the closing of a store, the fading of a mural—feels personal. The city becomes a kind of antagonist, not through violence, but through its refusal to acknowledge what the character has dared to feel.

Example: A teenage boy finally gathers the courage to come out—but the gay bar that made him feel seen just closed. The condo that will replace it is already being framed in steel. His personal breakthrough collides with the city's quiet erasure of what once sustained him.

Push, pull, pressure

Whether arcs align or oppose, the key is movement. City arcs gain strength when they carry force—when they exert pressure.

- If the city is blooming, does it lift your character? Or does it leave them behind?
- If the city is crumbling, does your character mourn it? Escape it? Pretend it isn't happening?
- If your character resists change, does the city punish or ignore them?
- If the city moves on without them, does your character chase it, fight it, or let themselves disappear?

These aren't metaphors. They're narrative levers. Allowing the city to evolve in tandem—or in tension—with a protagonist creates a dynamic world—one that feels lived in, layered, and urgent.

That pressure doesn't need to be dramatic. It might show up in the form of rising noise, shifting routines, a beloved place turning unfamiliar. But its effect on the character is profound: it asks them to adapt, withdraw, confront, or transform. When the city leans in—whether gently or with force—it reveals who the character is under stress. It brings contradictions to the surface. And it helps shape not just what happens, but how it feels.

Just like you choose whether a secondary character supports or challenges your protagonist, you can choose whether the city aligns with your character's arc—or resists it. Either choice builds tension.

Types of City Change You Can Use

Cities change in patterns—and those patterns shape story. Whether slow and creeping or sudden and explosive, urban transformation reshapes identity, power, belonging, and risk. When your fiction engages with how a city evolves, you're doing more than establishing a backdrop. You're building plot. You're shaping character. You're surfacing theme.

Here are four major types of city change—each with its own textures, tensions, and narrative fuel.

1. Gentrification and Economic Shift

The most visible and deeply contested transformation in many cities today. Gentrification isn't just real estate—it's story erosion. Ask:

- Who's moving in?
- Who's being displaced—and how is that loss marked, if at all?
- What gets renamed, rebranded, rebuilt?
- What symbols remain—and which are quietly erased?
- Who holds the narrative power—and whose version of the neighborhood becomes "official"?

116

Example: A corner store becomes a wine bar. The old signage is left up, but it's ironic now—aesthetic, not historical. A character walks past every day, wondering if anyone remembers the woman who used to run it, or the unofficial tab system that fed kids whose parents couldn't pay.

Economic shifts can surface themes of erasure, reinvention, alienation, shame, or rage. Gentrification isn't only about rent—it's about who gets to call a place home, and who gets written out of the story.

2. Environmental Change

Not speculative. Not future-tense. Already here. Cities are climate spaces now—strained, flooding, burning, breathing differently.

This change introduces material stakes:

- Heatwaves that shut down transit and kill seniors.
- A flood that cuts off a block from power—for a week.
- The first spring without the neighborhood garden blooming.

But also emotional stakes:

- What's it like to fall in love when the river you grew up skating on no longer freezes?
- How does it feel to build a future when every summer gets a little harder to breathe?
- What's it like to visit your childhood beach and find the shoreline barricaded, the sandbag wall covered in warning signs?

Example: A man proposes during a freak January thunderstorm. They're soaked. She says yes. But later that night, as she towels her hair dry and watches lightning flicker beyond the window, she wonders: *Is this weather—or warning? Is the sky celebrating—or trying to tell me something I missed?*

Environmental shifts make cities feel unstable, alive, threatened. They create urgency. They demand choices. They force characters to act.

3. Political Upheaval

Power shifts. Or pretends to. A new mayor comes in. A law changes. A curfew is declared. Police show up differently. Sometimes more. Sometimes not at all.

Political change isn't always sweeping or official. Sometimes it's a shift in who gets listened to, who gets policed, or whose presence is suddenly treated as a problem.

Political change turns a city into:

- A **battleground** (protests, counter-protests, curfews, street surveillance)
- A **refuge** (sanctuary spaces, mutual-aid kitchens, hidden networks)
- A **theatre** (public reckonings, city hall speeches, performative resilience)

Example: Your character works at a library turned warming shelter. For weeks, nothing happens—just coffee and blankets. Then one night, someone draws chalk outlines of missing relatives on the front steps. The next morning, the city shuts the shelter down "for cleaning."

This is the city as actor in the story—complicating, escalating, resisting. Fiction that engages with power systems doesn't always need a podium. What it needs is detail. Consequence. Pressure

4. Cultural Shift

Sometimes change isn't visible in structures—but in sound, ritual, rhythm, and memory.

- A local holiday disappears from the calendar.
- A public celebration returns for the first time since a crackdown.
- A block that once hummed with live jazz now plays ambient lo-fi from boutique speakers.
- A favorite food truck disappears, replaced by something trendier—with no smell, no music, no banter.

These changes seem small, but they often reveal deeper shifts in who the city thinks it's for—and who it quietly pushes out.

Example: A teenager hears his native language in public for the first time in months—not from his family, but over a new loudspeaker in the park. It's a new performance space. Sponsored by a bank. The voice feels familiar. But the context has changed.

Cultural change is subtle, sensory, and deeply personal. Use it when you want your characters to feel joy, loss, dissonance—or when they realize they're becoming strangers to their own city.

Putting It All Together

City change is layered. Often, these types intersect.

- A public housing tower comes down—and so does the basketball hoop that anchored the block.
- A neighborhood gets rebranded—and also floods more often.
- A new light rail opens—and the shops it once passed are gone.
- A mural gets commissioned to honor the neighborhood's roots—but the artist has never lived there.
- The skyline grows—but the shadows fall differently on the playgrounds below.
- A tech campus opens downtown—and the old bus route stops running on time.

You don't have to write a manifesto. But fiction begins with attention. Cities change—and your characters feel those changes in their lungs, their rent checks, their social lives, their silences.

The question is never just: what happens to the city? It's: What happens to your character because of what happens to the city?

When Stasis Becomes Story

Not all transformation is mutual. Sometimes the character evolves—and the city stays the same. That, too, is a kind of story. One marked by friction, heartbreak, clarity, or loss.

The buildings don't fall. The skyline holds. The rhythms of daily life go on. But the protagonist sees it all differently now. And that shift—that internal rupture in perception—is no less powerful than a protest or a flood.

Cities don't have to physically change to act on your character. They can exert pressure through refusal—by staying still while your character grows restless, wise, wounded, awake.

- A woman returns to her old neighborhood after twenty years and finds it untouched—the same stoplights, the same diner booths, the same broken bench by the river. But now the familiar feels eerie. The stillness is no longer comforting. It's oppressive.
- A teenager comes out and sees their neighborhood differently. The rainbow flags in the corner bar window suddenly feel fake. The laughter on the block now sounds like judgment. Nothing visible has changed—but everything has.
- A man who once loved the city for its grit—the corner hustle, the buskers, the smoke—now sees only exhaustion. The beauty hasn't disappeared. But he no longer wants to belong to it.

Not every story tracks a changing city. Some track a changing gaze—a character finally seeing the city for what it is, or what it's never been. That clarity can be painful—or liberating. It can reveal a rot they once ignored, or a grace they never noticed. It can force a decision: to stay and change the terms of survival, or to leave and carry the city with them anyway.

This emotional rupture hits hardest when:

- The character once loved the city deeply
- The city has protected its image at the expense of its people
- The city has become a symbol—and the symbol is cracking

Example: A schoolteacher walks the same route home every night, past the same mural of the city's "heroes." One day, a student tags a message over it: *We're still waiting.* She doesn't paint over it. She doesn't report it. She just stands there, reading. The mural hasn't changed. But now she sees what it always lacked.

But sometimes, the resistance isn't internal. Sometimes, it's the city itself that holds its ground—and pushes back.

When Cities Resist Change

Not all cities are eager to evolve. Some cities double down. Others calcify. Some rewrite the same story over and over—even when it no longer fits the people living inside it.

Cities resist change in different ways:

- Through institutional refusal—laws that don't adapt, policies that reinforce the past
- Through cultural conservatism—rituals that exclude, nostalgia that becomes a weapon
- Through deliberate forgetting—the refusal to name what happened, or who it happened to

When your character wants transformation—and the city won't allow it—that's not just atmosphere. That's narrative heat. That's plot.

This kind of resistance produces characters who must push, question, or survive inside hostile systems. The tension isn't just symbolic—it's embodied.

- **A queer teen in a conservative religious city:** Their existence is labeled a disruption. Even small joys—a kiss on the sidewalk, a pronoun correction, a rainbow pin—become acts of defiance. The city doesn't need to arrest them. Its silence is pressure enough. They don't want to burn it all down. They just want to be visible. And the city keeps looking away.
- **A progressive activist in a post-conflict city obsessed with forgetting:** The war is "over," and the official story is reconciliation. But statues still stand.

121

Archives are still sealed. Every attempt to remember is framed as provocation. The activist isn't looking for vengeance—just truth. And truth is what this city fears most.

- **A refugee in a city that doesn't want to see them:** They navigate a world that praises its diversity but closes every door. Their accent becomes a liability. Their food gets photographed and praised as "authentic," but not truly respected. Their labor is welcomed, but their grief isn't. The city says "you are welcome"— but it means "stay invisible."

These are stories of pushback. Of protagonists who demand to live fully in cities that only allow partial lives.

Example: A young woman starts a free clinic in a neighborhood abandoned by official funding. At first, the city ignores her. Then it tries to regulate her. Then it sends in developers to "revitalize" the area—displacing her patients in the process. She realizes: the city doesn't want restoration. It wants reinvention—even at the cost of erasure.

Cities as Antagonists—But Never Villains

It's easy to write a city as the villain. But cities are rarely that simple. Cities aren't evil. They're complex systems made of memory, policy, fear, and hope. When they resist change, it's usually to protect something—identity, power, myth, capital. So instead of asking:

- Why is this city cruel?
- Why won't this place change?
- Why does the city keep hurting people like my character?

Try asking instead:

- What is it afraid of losing?
- Who built it this way—and why?
- What comfort depends on keeping it this way?
- What would it take to make it yield?

These kinds of questions can give your story texture and urgency—especially when your character starts to answer them with action, or with rage, or with refusal.

Sometimes your protagonist runs up against a city that won't yield. They want more than the city is willing to give. They try to break the script.

But not all cities are willing participants in a character's arc. Some double down. Some close their fists. This can create powerful, high-stakes fiction.

- A queer teen trying to live freely in a city ruled by shame.
- A returning resident trying to replant roots in a neighborhood that no longer makes room.
- An undocumented worker navigating a city that depends on their labor but denies them recognition.
- A second-generation immigrant who wants to build something new—but the city only wants nostalgia.
- A single mother fighting to keep her apartment as rents double and school buses stop running.

When a character wants transformation, but the city won't budge—that's tension. That's story.

Because when cities resist change and characters demand it, your fiction gains teeth. And stories with teeth don't just describe the world. They leave a mark.

City Stories Don't Tie Up Neatly

At the end of your novel, the question isn't just: What happened? It's: What's still happening?

Cities rarely offer clean conclusions. They don't wrap themselves in ribbon or yield to narrative closure. Their rhythms outlast your plot. Their tensions persist beyond your final page. And that's not a failure of storytelling—that's a feature of what makes city-based fiction feel true.

Still, endings matter. And how your novel ends—emotionally, thematically, spatially—says everything about what you believe a city is.

To deepen your ending, consider:

- **Has the city changed?** Even subtly? Has a skyline shifted, a law passed, a mural gone up or come down?
- **Does your character perceive it differently?** Even if the city looks the same, does it feel changed—heavier, brighter, thinner, unfamiliar?
- **What's been destroyed, reclaimed, renamed?** And who did the destroying, the reclaiming, the renaming?
- **What cycles continue, undisturbed?** Gentrification. Invisibility. Silence. Celebration. Resistance. What carries forward?

Some stories end with transformation. Others with survival. Others with a character choosing to stay and fight, or finally walk away. All are valid. What matters is resisting the temptation to make the city a backdrop that can be "resolved."

Cities don't resolve. They churn. They pulse.

They keep going.

In Summary

Cities are always moving—sometimes forward, sometimes backward, sometimes in circles. They rise and fall, erase and remember, bloom and barricade.

This chapter invited you to see the city's transformation not as backdrop, but as story—where change becomes tension, power, resistance, and echo.

A city's arc can:

- Mirror your character's growth
- Counter it with sharp friction
- Expose what your character wants to ignore
- Refuse to bend, forcing your character to break—or break free

Not all change is visible. Sometimes the city shifts in mood, in perception, in what it allows or forbids. Sometimes the only shift is your character's ability to see clearly.

Cities aren't just environments. They are narrative engines.

They change. They resist. They become. Allow your fiction feel the weight of that motion.

Exercise 1: Parallel Arcs

Prompt: Cities change—and so do people. But those changes don't always move in sync. This exercise offers a way to map a character's emotional arc alongside the city's transformation, revealing points of tension, contradiction, or resonance.

Step 1: Sketch the Arcs

Draw a horizontal timeline—a week, a season, a year. On the vertical axis, track two arcs:

The **protagonist's emotional journey**
(rage → numbness → clarity)

The **city's state**
(indifference → unrest → renewal, etc.)

Step 2: Identify Tension Points

Look for three points where the arcs:

- **Intersect** (e.g., both protagonist and city in collapse)
- **Contradict** (e.g., the city heals while the character hardens)

Step 3: Rewrite One Scene

Choose one of those tension points and reimagine a scene so that the city's change actively pressures or deepens the character's emotional shift.

Bonus Prompt: The character may misread the city at first. Their understanding of its transformation might be incomplete, emotional, subjective—until something breaks.

Sample Answer (Chicago – Humboldt Park)

Isa stands on the platform at Western Avenue, clutching a folder of immigration paperwork that still smells like photocopier heat. Below, the street's loud with construction—the old bakery is being gutted, and she can't tell yet if that's relief or grief. When she moved here, the bakery gave out pan de coco and knew her daughter's name. Now it's all fencing and renderings and a banner that says *Coming Soon: Studio Flats with a Latin Flavor.* She tries to smile at the irony, but it doesn't come. She boards the Blue Line and doesn't look back.

What's happening:
City's arc: economic shift → cultural dissonance
Character's arc: hopeful determination → confusion → quiet mourning

The tension lies in contradiction: Isa is trying to build a future in a place that's already forgotten her past.

Exercise 2: Tilt the Scene

Prompt: Start a finished or in-progress scene from your story. Then revise it in one of the following ways:

- Place the city **in transition**—a protest just ended, a storm is beginning, a beloved store is closing.
- Let the **character's perception of the city shift**—from comfort to dread, from nostalgia to clarity.
- Or allow the **city to refuse to change**, and let that refusal create pressure.

Write a paragraph that reflects this shift—then add a sentence describing how it alters the emotional tone or tension of the scene.

This exercise brings the chapter's ideas down to the paragraph level—ideal for writers revising existing work or looking to intensify emotional stakes through place.

Sample Answer (Chicago – South Loop)

Original: Naomi walks to the pharmacy at State and Roosevelt, her hoodie up against the wind. It's quiet. Her ankle still hurts from the fall last week. She's not sure why the pain's worse at night.

Revised: Naomi rounds the corner and nearly walks into a barricade. The pharmacy's boarded up—windows shattered, plywood tagged in fresh silver paint: *No Justice, No Peace.* The protest must've swept through last night. She steps back, suddenly aware of how empty the street is. She feels the bruise in her ankle again—and something heavier she can't name pressing into her chest.

What changed: The tone shifted from quiet isolation to tension and unease. The city's unrest enters the scene and turns Naomi's private pain into something connected, and less safe.

Sample Answer 2 (Chicago – West Side):
Original: Andre waits for the bus at his usual stop on Pulaski. The bench is cracked, the schedule sign faded. He scrolls his phone, then pockets it, watching a stray plastic bag blow down the sidewalk. He doesn't expect the bus to be on time.

Revised: Andre waits at the same stop on Pulaski, just like he did before the funeral. The bench is still cracked. The schedule sign is still faded. The bus is still late. Nothing's changed—not the route, not the sidewalk, not the faces of the men on the corner. But now the silence feels heavier. His brother is gone, but the block doesn't flinch. The city just shrugs and keeps moving like it always does, and Andre doesn't know what to do with that.

What changed: The emotional tone shifted from resignation to grief. The city's refusal to change or acknowledge loss amplifies Andre's disorientation and deepens his sense of invisibility.

9

Beyond Flatness:
Writing Place with Depth and Integrity

You can feel it when a city on the page hasn't been fully imagined. The place feels decorative, borrowed. A skyline described at sunset—but never felt at street level. Neon on wet pavement, a saxophone echoing through an alley, a cat slipping beneath a rusted gate—evocative, yes, but unattached. The city becomes mood. Costume. A surface.

Sometimes this happens when a writer hasn't spent enough time in the city. Other times, it's because they haven't paused to question which version of the city they're drawn to—and why. Either way, the result can be the same: the story floats above the concrete.

This isn't about gatekeeping who gets to write what. It's about depth. Care. Nuance. Fiction that oversimplifies place tends to strip dimension from other things too—character, conflict, tension, truth.

This chapter gathers threads from earlier in the book—place as power, the city as provocation, the ethics of representation—and pushes them toward a final question: what does it mean to write place with integrity, especially when it isn't your own?

This chapter isn't a checklist. It's a deeper reflection on the ethics and craft of representing cities. Because when a place is rendered without contradiction, without weight, or without awareness of who's telling the story—and from where—it can unintentionally erase or appropriate more than it illuminates

But if you get it right—if you write the city with depth, friction, intimacy—you can build fiction that resonates far beyond the map.

When Aesthetic Replaces Depth

Fiction often sets itself in cities like Bangkok, Buenos Aires, Istanbul, Prague, or Nairobi—not because the story demands it, but because the writer is drawn to a certain feel: grit, edge, heat, history, or photogenic disrepair.

But what often emerges is a kind of borrowed aesthetic: a city that looks authentic but feels hollow. The street names are accurate. The food is described. Maybe there's even a wedding procession or festival in the streets. But the narrative never lives there. It passes through. It gestures. It gathers.

The city becomes a set of borrowed textures—not a place with history, tension, memory, and grief.

Take Wicker Park, for example. It often appears in short stories and novels as a kind of shorthand for "artsy Chicago": record shops, dive bars, cheap rents, creative angst. But that version of the neighborhood largely belongs to the past. The Polish Triangle isn't punk anymore. The 24-hour diner is gone. Rents are high, stores are curated, and what looks like grit is more aesthetic than structural. Wicker Park didn't stay frozen in time—it changed. The question becomes: does your depiction reflect that change?

This isn't about where you're allowed to set your story. It's about how—and why—you write it the way you do.

Before you pick a city for its vibe, ask yourself:

- Why this place—for these characters, in this plot, with this emotional arc?
- What do I owe the real people who live here—and to those whose stories have been displaced or overlooked?
- Am I writing toward complexity—or convenience?

- Whose stories am I centering—and whose am I ignoring?
- How does this city complicate the story I'm trying to tell—rather than simply accommodate it?

Cities don't exist to serve our stories. They exist because people have built them, struggled for them, and shaped them over time. That's where the writing begins.

When Place Stays Shallow

How can you tell if your fictional city is doing meaningful narrative work? Here are a few signals worth noting:

- Heavy on adjectives, light on action: the city is gritty, chaotic, vibrant—but little actually happens in it.
- Characters act like tour guides: "Let me take you to the market," "This is the best taco stand in town."
- The city holds only one mood or stereotype: Lagos is loud. Buenos Aires is passionate. Detroit is crumbling. (Each city, of course, holds far more than its shorthand.)
- Nothing pushes back: the character moves through the space without tension, contradiction, or cost.

If the city never provokes, limits, exposes, or surprises, it may not yet be fully alive on the page. And if the people who live there appear only to set a mood, it might be worth asking: is this a world that breathes—or just one that's been arranged?

Writing Cities with Depth

1. Start from Within the City

Even if the city isn't your hometown, your writing can still reflect its internal logic—not just its surface. That means noticing how the city feels, how it functions, and how it remembers. You're not just describing place; you're decoding it.

Here Are Some Ways In

- **Read novels, poetry, and essays by locals.** Seek out writers whose perspectives reflect the city's complexity—not just its tourist economy or literary export. What doesn't get explained in these works is just as revealing as what does.
- **Listen to local radio, news, and street interviews—not just the official press.** What's argued about on call-in shows? What slang appears in regional ads? What's posted on community boards or in neighborhood forums?
- **If you're able to visit, go with the goal of noticing what often stays invisible to outsiders.** Where do people wait? Where do they avoid? What does silence mean here?
- **Notice what gets remembered—and what gets erased.** A historical plaque might commemorate a site of resistance—or whitewash it. A mural might show someone excluded from the history books. Street names, empty lots, and building scars can all carry narrative weight.

Craft-Level Application

This kind of research isn't just about getting things right. It's about building tension, texture, and interiority.

- How might a character's assumptions about the city be challenged over time?
- What friction arises when they move between neighborhoods, languages, or social spheres?
- What do they misread—and what does that reveal about them?
- What are people fighting about in this city—and what does that conflict look like on the ground?
- What truths does this city carry that outsiders might miss?

- Who is forgotten here—and who keeps forgetting them?
- What can my characters see—and what remains outside their awareness?

2. Write the City's Multiplicity

Cities are never one thing. Not in demographic makeup, not in mood, not in daily rhythm. Even in heavily segregated or gentrified places, multiplicity survives—just unevenly distributed. Fiction that collapses a city into a single trait, tone, or identity not only misrepresents the place—it leaves narrative depth on the table.

Here are some common reductions:

- A queer city becomes its nightlife.
- An immigrant city becomes its food stalls.
- A "tech city" becomes its apps and architecture.
- A "historic city" becomes its cobblestones and ruins.

These aren't wrong—but they're fragments. And if fragments go unchallenged, they can strip dimension from character, stakes, and settings alike.

Ways to Deepen the Texture

- **Shift who your characters notice.** If they always interact with the same social stratum, introduce a moment of crossing—by class, race, generation, gender, or language.
- **Include the ordinary alongside the iconic.** Tourist districts might glitter, but what does a payday line look like? A quiet Tuesday morning on a residential street? The backroom of a shop after hours?
- **Write contradiction into your scenes.** A high-end grocery beside a halfway house. A mosque across from a dog park. A protest passing a wedding. Juxtaposition builds realism—and tension.

- **Use multilingualism.** Signage, graffiti, announcements, or overheard conversation can reveal deep layering—especially if your character doesn't speak every language around them.

Craft-Level Application

- When a neighborhood has a reputation, filter it through character perspective. A "dangerous" street might be a sanctuary for one person and a source of fear for another.
- Architecture can hold contradiction. What's behind that sleek new facade? Who lives above the bar? The hidden floors matter.
- Difference shapes outcomes. What can your character do or not do in certain spaces? Who gets stopped, questioned, waved through, watched?

Cities are always multiple. Fiction that reflects that will feel richer, truer, and more alive on the page.

3. Stay Curious, Not Certain

You can't know a whole city. Even lifelong locals don't. Cities are dynamic, layered, and often contradictory. Writing them well isn't about mastery—it's about approach. Like any relationship, writing a city asks for curiosity, humility, and the willingness to be surprised.

The risk of certainty is control. When a narrator speaks with too much authority, the city becomes a closed system. But cities resist that. They sprawl. They interrupt. They talk back.

Strategies for Curiosity

- **Filter the city through character perspective.** Descriptions can carry blind spots, projections, biases, and gradual awakenings. Characters don't need to see the whole city—just their slice of it, honestly rendered.
- **Include moments of misreading.** A character might

believe a neighborhood is "up and coming," only to realize they're part of its displacement cycle. Another might misjudge a street's danger—or safety. These shifts build tension and growth.

- **Let your characters be wrong.** Not every character needs to narrate from a place of wisdom or clarity. Fiction thrives on discovery—especially when the city does the correcting.
- **Allow the city to interrupt the narrative.** A missed bus, a shift in weather, a chance encounter—each can redirect the story, not by plot but by place.

Craft-Level Application

- Curiosity creates movement. Ask: what new thing does my character learn about this place in this chapter?
- When describing a location, ask: what assumptions might the character be making? What might they be missing?
- Create narrative moments where place disrupts the story. A protest. A power outage. A street performance. A bureaucratic delay. Each can shift what a character understands about where they are.
- Small details can reveal big shifts—watch what catches your character's attention.

Writing Place at a Distance

If you're writing a place you didn't grow up in—that's okay. Fiction isn't about claiming ownership. What matters is how that distance is approached. When writers gloss over difference—or smooth it into stereotype—stories risk losing their edge.

You don't need to pass as local to write with authority. But you do need to write with honesty about what your characters do and don't know. That's where narrative richness lives. Distance isn't a flaw—it's a narrative condition, and it can sharpen observation when handled with care.

Ways to Navigate Outsider Status with Integrity

- **Write from the perspective of someone who doesn't fully belong.** An outsider character gives you room to acknowledge complexity without overreaching. Their missteps and misunderstandings can generate narrative tension—and allow the city to become a living force that challenges and shapes them.

- **Make distance part of the story.** Characters can misread cues, get lost, rely on others, or romanticize aspects of the city that locals reject. These moments don't diminish your authority—they build it by grounding your storytelling in specificity and stakes.

- **Focus on what your character is able to see**—texture, rhythm, and interaction. Avoid assuming full access to subcultures, histories, or coded spaces unless it's earned on the page. Let the rest remain shadow, silence, or slow revelation.

- **Allow local characters to carry truths your protagonist can't fully reach.** This isn't about turning them into wise teachers—it's about giving other perspectives narrative space without filtering them through the main character's lens. A roommate, co-worker, or neighbor can correct, resist, or reframe what the main character thinks they understand.

Craft-Level Application

- A foreign journalist covering a protest misunderstands a chant—and prints the wrong message. A local calls them out. That confrontation becomes a pivot in the story.

- A White grad student rents an apartment in a historically Black neighborhood. They think of it as "affordable." A neighbor describes it as "unfinished business."

- A romantic lead falls in love with a city—but only sees it by night. A morning encounter shifts everything.

These are not just plot devices. They're moments where positionality becomes craft—and where fiction gains its weight.

You don't have to be from a city to write it well. But it does ask for care, humility, and a grounded point of view. Place can exceed your character's grasp. Their lens might be partial. And the city can expand beyond what the story can fully hold.

Write the System, Not Just the Scene

Cities are built on hierarchy—not just ideologically, but physically. Power isn't just in city hall; it's in bus routes, flood zones, and who gets to use the park after dark.

Where Power Hides in the Urban Fabric

- Zoning laws and school district lines
- Transit stops and their frequency
- Mortgage patterns and redlining ghosts
- Where benches go—and where barricades do instead
- Which languages appear on signage, warnings, graffiti, or shopfronts

These elements aren't backdrop—they're part of the plot.

Craft-Level Application

- A character waits twenty minutes for a bus while another hails a cab with ease. That's not just transportation—it's character contrast and spatial inequality.
- One character sees a quiet park as safe; another avoids it at all costs. The difference creates tension—and reveals history.
- A luxury condo rises where a family business used to stand. Your character might pass it without notice—or be haunted by what's missing. That silence can carry narrative weight.
- A character avoids calling an ambulance because they

137

don't trust who might arrive. That silence isn't just personal—it's systemic.

You don't need to write a political novel. But your novel already lives in political space. Characters move through systems whether they know it or not.

Systems shape more than movement. They influence:

- Who rests—and who runs
- Who's protected—and who's pursued
- Who sees the skyline—and who sees a billboard's back
- What gets named, and what stays forgotten

Even writing around the edges of power matters. Maybe your protagonist never sees the police station on the corner—because they've never needed to. Maybe they don't wonder why snow always gets cleared on their street but not the next. Those gaps? They're narrative material.

In cities, every sidewalk is a story of decisions. And every story walks through systems—even if the character doesn't see them.

A Framework for Writing Cities with Integrity

You don't need to master every detail of a city to write it well. But approaching it with depth, humility, and narrative intention can shape what the story becomes. Here's a flexible framework to guide your choices:

- **Specificity over Aesthetic:** Don't lean on visual shorthand. Write the city as a layered place—where details reveal relationships, tensions, and stakes.
- **Perspective over Panorama:** Filter the city through your characters. What they notice—and what they miss—can shape the world. The goal isn't total explanation, but a city that feels lived-in.
- **Complexity over Convenience:** Avoid single-tone depictions. Let contradictions live on the page. Every city holds multitudes—your fiction should too.

- ▸ **Systems over Surface:** Even quiet stories rest on structures of power. Zoning, transit, housing, surveillance—these systems shape who moves, who stays, who vanishes. They don't need to dominate the page to shape the world.
- ▸ **Change over Stasis:** Cities transform—characters' relationships to them can shift too. The city might challenge, correct, or reshape what your characters believe. It might even talk back.

This isn't a checklist. It's a mindset: write with awareness, not assumption. Think of the city not as backdrop, but as presence—as force.

In Summary

Writing cities well means refusing to flatten them. It means writing with depth, specificity, humility, and tension. Cities are contradictory. They hold multitudes. They hurt and heal. It's not just about avoiding cliché—it's about engaging place as a layered, living force. That means:

- ▸ Treating place as more than aesthetic
- ▸ Portraying lives as more than mood or texture
- ▸ Approaching cities—even unfamiliar ones—with care, curiosity, and narrative intention

It means noticing who's centered—and who's erased. It means tracking movement, access, conflict, change. It means recognizing when the city challenges your character's assumptions—and letting that friction reshape the story.

Write the block that argues with itself. The storefront with five sets of hours taped to the window. The banner that celebrates a future not everyone survives to see. Write what your character misreads—and how the city responds.

Exercise: Five Perspectives, One Block

Prompt: Choose a single city block. Now describe it five different times—each from the perspective of a different character:

- A rideshare driver
- A teenager skipping school
- A city planner
- A recent immigrant
- A long-time resident watching the block change

Each version shifts based on:

- What the character notices
- What they value
- What they fear or avoid

The goal isn't just variety—it's contradiction. A single block might feel safe, threatening, beautiful, or broken depending on who's moving through it. Place bends under different gazes. And that difference? That's the story.

Sample Answer (Chicago: 18th Street, Pilsen)

Rideshare driver: Sees the street in terms of time and hazard—"one-way hell," potholes by the viaduct, tight turns near the taco trucks. Doesn't look up at the murals anymore.

Teenager skipping school: Eyes dart for familiar faces, cops, crushes, and trouble. The block is a map of risks and thrills. The corner store sells single cigarettes under the counter. The alley is sacred ground.

City planner: Reads traffic flow, zoning contradictions, curb cuts that don't meet ADA. Doesn't register the people—just potential: "revitalization corridor," "streetscape modernization," "mixed-use overlay."

Recent immigrant: Feels between languages. The church sign is in Spanish, the new café menu is not. Notices who nods hello, and who looks through her. Her toddler always stops to wave at the man fixing bikes on the corner.

Long-time resident: Walks slowly. Remembers what used to be here—the bakery, the music store, the cousin's auto shop. Keeps a mental inventory of what's gone. Doesn't say much. Sees everything.

10

The Emotional Logic of Urban Survival

The city doesn't just shape what's possible. It shapes what feels safe.

By now, we've explored the city as system, as memory, as constraint, as catalyst. We've seen how architecture, infrastructure, rhythm, and inequality shape the plot. But there's a more intimate layer beneath all of it: the emotional patterns city life produces—how it conditions the psyche to respond to pressure, threat, loneliness, opportunity, or desire.

This chapter isn't about what a city looks like. It's about what it teaches people to feel. Because cities don't just govern access to housing, transit, or clean air. They govern internal weather. They generate emotional habits. They script what's dangerous, what's desirable, and what's delayed. They teach people how to mask grief, perform resilience, navigate intimacy, and protect their own pulse in public.

Urban life—especially for those without power—requires adaptation. And that adaptation becomes emotional logic. By logic, I don't mean cold calculation. I mean pattern—what makes emotional sense under pressure, when choice is shaped by space.

A boy learns not to linger. A woman learns not to ask for softness. A teenager learns to love behind closed doors, fast and temporary, because the sidewalk doesn't welcome their touch. A man learns that to

141

survive is to stay watchful—even when no one is watching.

These aren't quirks of personality. They're conditioned responses to a pressurized environment. They are survival strategies etched into the body. And fiction, if it's going to write the city honestly, must learn to track them.

Cities Teach the Body to Flinch

Every city teaches lessons about what to expect from people, from institutions, from the future.

Some cities train people to be alert. Others to be numb. In some places, visibility is a liability. In others, invisibility is the cost. The emotional habits people carry—guardedness, urgency, code-switching, wariness of trust—aren't arbitrary. They're often built into the grid.

A public bench split by dividers signals that rest isn't allowed. A police tower on your block tells you that you're already presumed suspicious. A school closing tells you where dreams are allowed to grow— and where they aren't.

These signals are constant, even when they're silent. And people respond to them—not always consciously, but consistently.

They build patterns:

- Don't stay too long.
- Don't get too close.
- Don't expect permanence.
- Don't rely on systems.
- Don't be visible unless you're invulnerable.
- Don't show need unless you can disguise it as strength.
  Don't mistake temporary access for belonging.

You see this in city love stories—fleeting, private, wary. In city ambition—strategic, contingent, hungry. In city grief—subterranean, unsanctioned, metabolized in movement.

It's not that people in cities don't feel deeply. It's that some of them have learned where it's safe to feel—and where it's not.

And that shapes the story before a word of dialogue is ever written.

Emotional Patterns That Aren't Personality

Writers often treat character emotion as interior or innate—grief, fear, avoidance, need. But in cities, many of these patterns are environmental. They're not internal states. They're adaptations.

And they're not just personal. They're collective. Emotional logic in the city doesn't live only in one person's nervous system—it's often shared, rehearsed, and reinforced within families, neighborhoods, and blocks. On the West Side, a grandmother teaches her grandsons how to carry themselves through a store. On the South Side, whole communities grieve together in rhythms the city doesn't always see. In Little Village, mutual aid isn't a trend—it's a memory system. Emotional logic is passed down not through advice, but through gesture, silence, side-eyes, rituals. Cities don't just shape individuals. They shape us—collectively.

If you want to write the city honestly, write what it teaches people to do with emotion.

1. Guardedness Isn't Coldness. It's Skill

In Chicago, survival often depends on how well you can read a room. Or a bus. Or a block.

You don't make eye contact on the Red Line after midnight—not because you're unfriendly, but because you've learned not to invite attention you can't control. You don't show grief on the platform because it's not the place for it. You walk fast, headphones in, shoulders tense—not because you're cold, but because the city taught you to be efficient with your vulnerability.

The urban nervous system adapts fast. Your character might brush someone off, ghost a friend, delay saying I love you—not because they're emotionally unavailable, but because they've internalized that softness has a price. And in Chicago, that price might be steep.

2. Distance Isn't Disinterest. It's Survival Logic

People in cities learn to leave early: relationships, leases, jobs, versions of themselves. If something feels temporary, you don't invest too

143

much. If people disappear often, you learn not to hold on too tightly. If stability feels conditional—based on rent, weather, violence, gentrification—then love becomes a thing you touch fast, but don't grip.

A woman living in a Pilsen walk-up might keep her boxes packed. Not because she's transient, but because she knows the building just sold. Again. A teenager in Englewood might not tell their crush how they really feel, because they've learned that vulnerability attracts risk. A man in Rogers Park might never meet his neighbors—because every lease feels one winter away from eviction.

This isn't trauma. It's logic. A logic built by the city.

Of course, Chicago isn't one story. It's a grid of contradictions. These examples aren't definitive—but they reflect how specific neighborhoods shape specific behaviors, especially under pressure.

Every city does this, but Chicago teaches in a very particular dialect—one built on history, code, and contradiction.

Chicago rewards performance. It does not reward openness. It tells you to be tough. Not tender. To be loyal. But not naive. To love the block—but never too loudly, never too long, because the block might disappear under a developer's sign next week.

Visibility as Risk

In Northalsted, a queer couple might walk hand-in-hand on Halsted, but drop it the second they hit Wrigleyville on Addison—just a few blocks, but a different social grammar. On the South Side, a Black teenager knows which hoodie gets them followed in Hyde Park and which gets ignored in Chatham. Visibility here is conditional. Who sees you—and how—is shaped by neighborhood, time, body, posture.

Your characters should feel that tension. A moment of silence in a Jewel-Osco aisle might carry the weight of a thousand micro-decisions: Do I explain who I am? Do I stay small? Do I make eye contact? Do I perform being from here—or let the city make me prove it?

Movement as Safety or Exposure

The Blue Line might offer escape to the Loop—but only if your shoes don't mark you as from the wrong side of the Milwaukee/Western divide—where the neighborhood vibe and social read can shift abruptly. The Red Line from 95th Street to the North Side might take an hour—but it crosses two lives: the one you live at home, and the one you invent at school. Fiction needs to feel those journeys. Not just in space—but in how the body contracts or expands across the route.

What does the city do to someone's capacity to stay soft?

In Chicago, the answer depends on ZIP code, bus transfer, time of day, and whether someone on the other side of the turnstile sees you as human.

Ambition, Intimacy, and Deviance Under Pressure

The city doesn't just shape how people guard themselves. It shapes how they chase. What they hope for. What they give up on.

Some of that gets called personality. Some gets labeled pathology. But when you widen the lens, you start to see a deeper truth: people navigate the city—emotionally and behaviorally—with the logic of someone surviving a system they didn't design.

This isn't metaphor. It's pattern. And fiction needs to see the difference.

Ambition looks different depending on where the bus stops

In a city like Chicago, even ambition is spatial.

A high school student in Roseland might want to go to college—but the nearest after-school program closed last year. Their counselor is juggling a caseload of 300. Their parents work two jobs. There is no legacy, no shortcut, no room for error. Every step takes longer. And every delay costs more.

Compare that to a teen in Lincoln Park who can walk to three internship sites, gets a laptop in 9th grade, and doesn't think twice about asking for a letter of recommendation—because that's always been the language of their neighborhood.

Same city. Different architecture of possibility.

So when you write a character who hesitates, who self-sabotages, who plays small—ask if that's really personality. Or if it's the residue

145

of a city that taught them not to expect access.

And when you write ambition, don't default to hunger. Write fatigue. Write a dream that's been contorted so many times to fit the grid, it barely resembles what it once was.

Love moves differently across train lines

Urban love is rarely slow. And even when it's deep, it's often compressed, accelerated, secret, or temporary. The reasons aren't always emotional. They're infrastructural.

What do you do when the person you love lives in a different neighborhood, and your ID doesn't match your name or gender, and the Blue Line is running late again, and the park where you used to meet now feels policed?

You adapt. You meet indoors. You touch quickly. You don't post photos. You don't plan more than a week ahead.

That's not detachment. It's design logic.

You love the way the city allows: fast, clever, occasionally distorted. You build closeness in short bursts and borrowed time. Because you've learned that access to closeness is conditional. And you can't afford to linger.

Sometimes love doesn't vanish—it just adapts beyond recognition. The calls get shorter. The routes get longer. Desire doesn't disappear. It just finds new ways to hide—behind the glow of a screen, behind a train delay, behind a goodbye said too soon. The city doesn't end the romance. It reroutes it until it no longer arrives on time.

Your fiction should reflect that. A romance might falter—not because the feelings weren't real, but because the infrastructure broke first. A character might choose the person who lives closer to the train. Another might choose solitude—not out of independence, but because it costs too much to feel that exposed again on a bus at 11:30 p.m.

Maybe they stop meeting halfway because the halfway point never feels neutral. Maybe they reroute their commute to avoid the block where they kissed for the first time. The city doesn't forget. It marks you. Sometimes it makes you walk a little farther just to feel safe again.

This is emotional logic. Shaped by the grid. And it's how many real people love in cities like this one.

Deviance isn't rebellion, it's logic

A man boosts a car in Back of the Yards—not because he's reckless, but because every job interview he's gotten in the last six months required a background check and a clean address, and he has neither.

A kid sells weed in Little Village—not because he's chasing glamor, but because the nearest grocery store closed, his cousin's been incarcerated for two years, and the family needs cash more than character endorsements.

A mother commits housing fraud—not because she's unethical, but because the school across the street underperforms by every metric, and the one in another ZIP code might be her daughter's only shot at escaping what she couldn't.

These aren't exceptions, but patterns—predictable when you look at the structure that shaped them.

If urban sociology has shown us anything, it's that people behave in ways that reflect the options the city gives them. Not the ones it markets. The real ones. The ones that cost something. The ones you see on the walk home. The ones you learn not to name out loud.

Fiction has the same responsibility: to stop asking what's wrong with the character, and start asking what system they've been asked to survive—and at what cost.

When Survival Stops Working:
Burnout and the Buffer of Friendship

Emotional logic helps people survive the city. But what happens when even those strategies stop working?

Cities can demand so much alertness, so much performance, that the nervous system eventually dulls. The reflexes that once protected—guardedness, pace, withdrawal—start to calcify. What once felt like adaptation can slowly become disconnection. You stop flinching. You stop noticing. Not because things got easier—but because your emotional bandwidth collapsed.

This is burnout. Not dramatic, not explosive—just slow erosion. A character doesn't need to cry on the train to show collapse. Maybe they stop answering messages. Maybe they turn off the noise, and keep it off. Maybe they walk a familiar block and feel nothing. Even silence used to mean something. Now it's just static.

Fiction set in cities should make space for that kind of numbness. For the character who isn't surviving well. For the moment survival becomes silence.

But if emotional logic breaks under pressure, it can also be rebuilt in community. Not always through romance. Often through friendship—through chosen family, mutual care, quiet interdependence. In cities, these relationships aren't soft. They're architectural.

A friend brings you soup when your EBT didn't reload. Someone gives you the couch key without asking questions. A neighbor covers your shift. A cousin walks you home. These gestures aren't extra. They're what make survival strategies sustainable. They're where emotion gets to be safe again—briefly, and not always evenly, but enough.

Your fiction can reflect that too. How people buffer against burnout. How friendship becomes infrastructure. How someone stays alive in the city because one person kept showing up.

Writing the City's Emotional Blueprint

Urban survival isn't just atmospheric. It's embodied. So when you're writing fiction set in cities—especially cities like Chicago—your characters' emotional responses, habits, and hesitations should be shaped by place as much as by past.

What follows isn't a checklist. It's a reframing. A way to write character not just as a container of feeling, but as a person negotiating emotional survival in terrain designed to pressure, deny, or redirect them.

1. Replace Traits with Conditions

Instead of asking, What kind of person is she? Ask, What has this city asked her to carry? To conceal? To adapt to?

- Maybe she avoids intimacy because she's learned it's not safe to want anything the city can take away.
- Maybe he overworks not out of ambition, but because rest has never felt safe—socially or otherwise.

- Maybe they code-switch—not for belonging, but for protection.
- Maybe she second-guesses every compliment—because in her neighborhood, praise usually came right before something was taken away.

Traits are static. Conditions are responsive. The more your characters' emotions emerge from specific, lived environments, the more credible they become.

2. Reframe Perception Through Place

The same block can feel like freedom to one person and danger to another.

A street in Humboldt Park might smell like home to a kid who grew up there—but to someone priced out and pushed west, it might sting of betrayal. A walk down 47th might feel like nothing to a long-time resident. But to a newcomer trying to navigate their first week, it might buzz with coded language they haven't yet learned.

Perception in fiction is never neutral. Your characters might misread the city at first. Their emotional logic may shift over time. They'll flinch, then relax, then overcorrect. As experience builds, it reshapes their internal landscape—and alters what they believe about who they are, what's possible, and what the city demands of them.

3. Map Emotion onto the Grid

In real life, emotion is spatial. So in fiction, let location encode memory and meaning.

- The alley behind the corner store isn't just an alley—it's where he first ran from the cops.
- The stairs outside her grandmother's Bronzeville apartment don't just creak—they sound like absence.
- The quiet street she walks in North Center isn't peaceful—it's eerie, because peace has never been ambient for her.
- The footbridge over the expressway isn't scenic—it's

where her thoughts start to spiral.

- The bus shelter outside the high school isn't a place to wait—it's where he last saw his brother, and now he can't stand still there.

- The crosswalk in front of the liquor store isn't just a shortcut—it's where she froze the night she found out he was gone, and she hasn't walked through it since.

These details aren't just flavor. They are emotional infrastructure. Your fiction can treat them like emotional muscle memory.

If your protagonist flinches every time they hit a particular corner, don't explain it in exposition. The city can trigger it. The physical space can act as a co-narrator. The reader should feel the pressure as much as the character does.

4. Use Delay, Evasion, and Small Decisions as Emotional Truth

Characters shaped by urban pressure often reveal themselves indirectly.

Instead of saying "I miss you," they might check which train stop someone gets off at. Instead of admitting fear, they might scan the sidewalk before unlocking their bike. Instead of pursuing a dream, they might say: I don't think that's for me.

In Chicago, especially, where pride is often armor and survival is posture, emotional truth shows up in:

- Who gets the address—and who's told to just "meet there"
- Who gets buzzed up—and who's met at the gate
- Who gets walked home
- Who gets a seat near the window
- Who gets a copy of the key

Track those details. That's where the emotional logic of urban life lives—not in confessions, but in pattern. In gesture. In delay. In disappearance.

When the City Isn't Yours (Yet): Writing the Outsider

Some characters arrive in the city already shaped by it—born into its noise, alert to its tempo, fluent in its spatial rhythm. Others are dropped into it.

Whether it's a transplant, a returner, a drifter, a newcomer from another country or suburb, or someone fleeing something quieter, the city won't greet them softly. And if it does, they might want to ask why.

If emotional logic is local knowledge, then your outsider doesn't have it yet. And that gap creates narrative electricity.

They might:

- Smile too often on the train, and get avoided.
- Assume friendliness means trust, and misread it as intimacy.
- Offer vulnerability in a place that requires proof before tenderness.
- Speak loudly in a space where silence is a signal.
- Ask questions locals stopped answering years ago.

An outsider's first mistake isn't usually arrogance. It's assumption. They assume friendliness means openness. That a clean sidewalk means safety. That an invite means belonging. They assume that what worked in their last city—or suburb, or small town—will translate here.

But cities like Chicago are fluent in difference. What you wear, how you speak, what time you move, what you notice—all of it gets read. And misread.

A newcomer might enter a bar in Logan Square and comment on the neighborhood's "authentic vibe"—not realizing they've stepped into a space where half the regulars were displaced by that same vibe five years earlier. They might try to interview a neighbor for a creative project—without realizing that in some neighborhoods, being observed is a form of threat.

And yet, the city isn't cruel. It's protective. The rules aren't arbitrary—they're cumulative. Built from history, damage, pride, and lived time.

When your outsider character fails, they don't just stumble. They uncover the city's emotional architecture. They find out which questions get answered and which don't. They learn to move through space not as a consumer of culture, but as a guest in someone else's home.

They should learn late. They might offend. They'll resist. And when they finally listen, the city might begin to speak. That's when they become legible—not by conquering the city, but by earning their place in its quiet choreography.

Writing the city means writing pressure. Writing response. Writing the choreography between what a person feels and what the city allows them to show.

That choreography deserves to be written clearly—stumbles and all. How the outsider navigates—fumbles, adjusts, performs, or resists—reveals who they are.

Chicago, Specifically

A character might move to Chicago thinking it's fast and glamorous—only to discover that its rules are unwritten but enforced. They might think Wicker Park still means artists. They might not know what the South Side means unless someone tells them—and even then, only halfway.

They might learn the hard way that some blocks talk back, and others just watch.

They might learn that you don't say "I'm from Chicago" unless you can name your cross street, your high school, your corner store. They might not realize that neighborhood allegiance isn't nostalgia—it's inheritance. It's defense.

They might get it wrong. That wrongness can create conflict. It can expose how much they're projecting—and how much the city withholds from those who haven't earned its rhythm.

Over time, maybe they start to learn: where to walk and where to listen. What not to ask. When to take the bus and when to wait for the train. Maybe they earn softness from a neighbor. Or get kicked out of a bar for assuming the vibe. Maybe they stop narrating the city and start listening to it.

But learning a city isn't always graceful. Some characters don't adapt—they fragment. The pressure to belong, to perform fluency, to hide unfamiliarity, can lead to unraveling. A wrong turn at night. A comment misunderstood. A refusal to acknowledge that the warmth they felt downtown doesn't stretch west of Ashland. The city isn't being cruel—it's being itself. But that can feel like cruelty when your internal map hasn't caught up yet.

The fear can be ambient. The embarrassment can live in the body. The risk of being seen—or not seen—can start to corrode their confidence. The city doesn't have to threaten them outright to make them question their place in it. Even the silence can destabilize them. Even the small things can tilt them off center.

And maybe the emotional logic of the city—its restraint, its heat, its pressure—starts to reshape them, too.

That's when fiction turns. When place stops being a background and starts becoming a force.

From Survival to Story

What the city builds into people—guardedness, urgency, ambition shaped by absence—isn't just background. It's structure. And when you start to write those emotional logics with intention, your fiction stops being atmospheric and starts becoming necessary. That's the next step. Not just understanding how the city shapes its people—but learning how to write those patterns into every choice, every silence, every beat of plot.

That's where we go next.

In Summary: City Pressure as Narrative Engine

Urban life builds people who are watchful, fast, strategic with intimacy, fluent in code, and loyal to what the city lets them keep. These are not quirks. They are survival tactics.

If your fiction is set in the city—but your characters act like space is neutral, like emotion moves freely, like power doesn't constrict the breath—they're not really urban characters.

If your characters fall in love in Chicago, they should be negotiating access. If they fight in New York, they should do it at volume and pace. If they grow up in Detroit, they should know what happens when a system stops pretending to care.

Write the emotional logic of the city not as flavor, but as friction.

The city should shape what your character wants—or what they've learned not to want. It can punish them for showing the wrong emotion in the wrong space. Softness may be withheld until it's earned—or demanded when it's unsafe to give.

And when an outsider arrives, they shouldn't inherit the city without resistance. They might misread. They might learn. They might choose what to keep and what to surrender.

Because the city isn't just setting. It's emotional design. And your characters aren't just reacting to space. They're surviving it.

Fiction set in the city should carry the weight of its sidewalks, its silences, and the systems that shape who gets to breathe freely.

As we move into the final chapter, we'll build a craft framework for exactly that: how to structure fiction so that cities act not just on setting—but on soul.

Exercise 1: Map a Character's Emotional Reflexes

Prompt: Choose a character from a story you're working on (or invent one). Describe three of their core emotional reflexes—automatic behaviors they exhibit under stress, fear, or intimacy. Then explain how the city they live in shaped each one.

This exercise is not about backstory. It's about adaptation. What does your character do emotionally that makes sense in their environment—even if it looks irrational from the outside?

Sample Answer

Reflex: She doesn't ask for help, even when overwhelmed.
→ Because her neighborhood has a culture of independence—the kind where asking means exposing a weakness that could be exploited.

Reflex: He memorizes license plates.
→ Because growing up near constant police surveillance taught him to track threats silently.

Reflex: They always sit near the exit at restaurants.

→ Because public space has never felt neutral. It's always required an escape plan.

Exercise 2: Write a Scene with Emotional Mismatch

Prompt: Write a short scene where an outsider misreads a local's emotional behavior. Show how the city has trained each character to respond differently to space, silence, and attention.

This is a tension exercise. Don't resolve the misunderstanding. Focus on the friction created by emotional logics shaped in different environments.

Sample Answer

A woman from a quiet suburb is visiting a friend in Uptown. She smiles at strangers and greets the cashier warmly. Her friend, who's lived there his whole life, gets tense. He's learned that friendliness can be read as instability or intrusion. She thinks he's rude. He thinks she's unsafe. Neither says it out loud.

Exercise 3: Design a Block That Builds Emotion

Prompt: Imagine a single block in a city—real or invented. Now describe what it teaches someone who lives there about love, fear, or belonging. Then, write a 100-word scene showing how a character behaves differently on this block than they would anywhere else.

The goal is to let architecture, visibility, rhythm, or history shape how the character moves, touches, or hides.

Sample Answer

Block: A narrow, dimly lit street between two new condo towers, still lined with three original brownstones. There's a broken light, a bus bench with dividers, and a camera mounted on a pole no one trusts.

Scene: Luis lights a cigarette with his back against the brick. He doesn't walk here—he waits. Hands in pockets. Eyes down. The street's too narrow for comfort, too wide to claim. He listens for footsteps but pretends not to. Doesn't call his boyfriend until he's on the next block. This one listens wrong. He can feel it—like something's missing. Or watching. It's not the danger. It's the pressure. Like the block is trying to remember who it used to belong to. And who it's supposed to police now. He exhales slow. Doesn't linger. Doesn't run. Just leaves before it names him.

11

Writing the City

Cities don't just hold your story. They shape it. They interrupt it. They escalate it. They punish it.

By now, you've learned to treat the city as more than setting. You've explored its rhythms, its power, its memory, its emotional logic. You've watched it haunt and heat and hollow out your characters. You've seen it remember things your characters would rather forget.

Now it's time to bring it all together. Not as summary, but as strategy.

This chapter offers a narrative outline: a flexible, repeatable way to build fiction that doesn't just take place in a city, but emerges from it.

But let's start with the central metaphor one more time—not because you've forgotten it, but because it needs sharpening: The city is a character.

Not just because it's moody or beautiful or has "personality." But because it has rules. And when those rules are broken—it responds.

Like any character, the city has:

- Desires and fears
- Triggers and scars
- Public masks and private codes
- Power, and ways of using it

And like any character with power, it can reward—or retaliate.

- The city might protect your protagonist—until they betray it.
- It might ignore them—until they demand to be seen.
- It might punish them for forgetting who it really serves.

A character violates the city's code—and a door closes. A job disappears. A street once safe becomes a trap.

You don't need to personify the city literally (though that would be interesting). You just need to write it with agency, memory, and teeth.

What follows isn't a checklist. It's a way of thinking. A way of building story from the ground up—street by street, wound by wound.

Let's begin.

The City as Emotional Blueprint

Before plot. Before character. Before conflict. Start with mood.

Not the city's "vibe"—but its emotional undercurrent. What it feels like to walk its streets. What lives between its buildings. What hums just under the noise.

Because the city isn't just where your story happens—it's what gives your story its temperature, its tone, its tension. Every narrative lives inside an emotional ecosystem. That ecosystem often begins with place.

So ask yourself:

- What does this city feel like? Anxious? Mournful? Arrogant? Hollow?
- Is it loud to cover something up? Quiet because it's watching?
- What is the dominant mood—and what's repressed beneath it?

A brittle city makes certain kinds of stories possible. A city that's grieving will bend characters differently than one that's smug or restless or terrified of its own future.

This doesn't mean everyone feels the same way about the place. Emotional resonance isn't uniform—but it is ambient. It gets into people. It shapes tone whether you name it or not.

Example: A novel set in a post-industrial river city might carry a slow, wet sadness. Streets sag with rust. The past is visible everywhere—in signage, in surface, in silence. But within that sadness, there's also intimacy. People know each other. Grief and closeness become the emotional baseline—not spectacle, but tension. And every narrative turn reverberates against that weight.

This mood doesn't need to be explained. It needs to be felt. Your first decision about place can be emotional. What is this city doing to the people inside it? What has it already done? And then—what will it do next?

Start with the City's Rules

Most stories start with a question: *What does my character want?*

In urban settings, you need a second question just as urgently: What does the city allow? And what does it punish?

Because cities aren't blank stages. They have rules—written and unwritten. They have limitations that shape character action, decision-making, even desire.

So instead of just asking, *What happens in this city?*—ask:

- Who is allowed to move freely—and who is not?
- What neighborhoods are accessible, and to whom?
- What happens when someone crosses an invisible line?
- What kind of change is welcomed—and what kind is crushed?

These are not side details. These are the limits of your story's world. They dictate what kind of transformation is possible—and what it will cost.

Example: In a story set in a city under increasing surveillance, your protagonist might long for intimacy—but every gesture is watched. A kiss in public is met with a fine. A second glance across a café becomes a risk The city isn't neutral. It's a system that governs possibility. And that system isn't broken—it's designed.

Cities as Systems of Constraint

In strong city-centered fiction, the structure of the place becomes the structure of the story.

A character's goal will come into tension with the city's reality.

The plot will be shaped by navigating—or failing to navigate—those tensions.

Even silence is strategic: what the city refuses to acknowledge becomes part of the narrative's constraint.

The city limits what your characters can do. It forces reroutes, delays, secrecy. It corners them. Wear them down.

A character wants to tell the truth—but the city doesn't allow speaking that truth in public. A character wants to escape—but there's only one bridge, and it's closed every night at six. A character wants to be seen—but the city only sees people like them when it's convenient or profitable.

This is where plot pressure lives. Not just in interpersonal conflict, but in the architecture of power. Your characters can want things the city won't give. Then make them face a choice: comply, resist, subvert—or break.

Design Around Friction

Cities are not smooth. They are jagged, layered, uneven. They are made of edges—and that's where your fiction should live.

Don't place your story in the city's center of comfort or order. Place it at the seams—where things rub, crack, spark.

Every city contains thresholds:

- ‣ Public / private
- ‣ Visible / invisible
- ‣ Welcome / excluded
- ‣ Historical / redeveloped
- ‣ Sacred / violated
- ‣ Gentrified / resisting

- ▸ Policed / abandoned
- ▸ Legal / lived

These aren't abstract binaries. They are real-world frictions with emotional, material, and narrative weight. And they change depending on who your character is and where they stand.

Example: A character crosses from one neighborhood into another—and the streetlight rhythm changes. The pace of pedestrians changes. The shop signage switches languages. A cop slows their car. The character keeps walking, trying to act like they belong. That moment isn't a tangent. It's friction—and it tells you what kind of story this is.

Fiction Belongs at the Edge

If the city is a system, its seams are where the system glitches. Where its promises get tested. Where the line between old and new, safe and unsafe, seen and unseen isn't fully drawn yet.

That instability is where narrative lives. Don't center the smooth street. Center the block with scaffolding. The corridor with mixed loyalties. The plaza where five different truths collide.

Fiction happens in contested space. That's where your characters have to choose who they are—and who they're willing to become.

Allow the story to breathe at the boundary. The city stretches or strains. Friction becomes structure.

Ask the City What It Remembers

Cities don't forget. They just change what they choose to recall—and what they bury.

As a writer, you already think about your characters' backstories. Their pasts shape their actions, fears, and desires. In city-centered fiction, it's worth asking: What is this city's backstory? What happened here—and who still feels it?

Every city has memory. Some of it is official: statues, street names, landmarks. Some of it is secret: stories passed down in kitchens, scars visible only to those who know where to look. Some memory is so present it haunts the sidewalk.

161

Your work isn't to recite history. It's to let the city's memory shape the atmosphere, the stakes, the tone. Ask:

- What wound in this city still throbs?
- What does the city remember—and who remembers differently?
- What's been erased on the map, but not in the body?
- What buildings have been repainted, but not forgotten?
- What silence still hums beneath the noise?
- What story does the city keep trying to bury—but it won't stay buried?

These aren't background questions. They're plot opportunities.

Example: A woman opens a café in a rapidly changing neighborhood. She doesn't know the building used to be a community health clinic. But her first customer walks in, stares at the corner wall, and goes silent. He used to sit there while waiting to hear if his brother would live. The room hasn't changed—not really. The walls still remember. And now the story does too.

Memory as Plot Pressure

The past can bleed into the present—subtly, atmospherically, suddenly, or loudly.

- A protest echoes an earlier one—same chants, same corner, new stakes.
- A character realizes they're living in the house where something went wrong.
- A park is built over a site no one mentions—except a child who starts drawing it.
- A seemingly kind policy mirrors an older, crueler one—just with better branding.

This isn't nostalgia. It's narrative continuity. It's what gives your fiction density, tension, and emotional risk.

Have the city remember something your character doesn't. Then let them walk into it—blind.

Give the City a Trajectory

Just like characters, cities change—or try not to. They grow. They rot. They recover. They lie. They name themselves new things. They forget old things on purpose.

Your story doesn't need to span decades to show this. Even in fiction that takes place over a day, the city can arc.

Maybe not visibly. But in pressure. In mood. In what becomes possible. The city itself has a narrative. And you can trace it—or interrupt it. Ask:

- What direction is the city moving in—socially, economically, spiritually?
- Is it trying to reinvent itself—and who's left behind in that process?
- Is it stuck in nostalgia—and who's suffocating inside the myth?
- Is it pretending to change—or resisting it outright?

That movement—or resistance—can shape how your characters move too.

Example: A city in the throes of "revitalization" launches a campaign: billboards declare a new future, train stations are rebranded, rents skyrocket. A longtime resident is trying to rebuild after personal loss—but every block they walk looks less like the place that held them and more like a future they were never invited into. The city is changing. The question is whether they can—or should—keep up.

Unfinished Cities, Unfinished Stories

Just like a character, a city doesn't need a clean ending.

- Maybe it starts to change—and the story ends before we see how.
- Maybe it doesn't change at all—and that's the heartbreak.
- Maybe it resists until the last page—and finally blinks.
- Maybe it makes room—but no one's left to take it.

163

Your job isn't to resolve the city. Your job is to show what happens when its trajectory meets your character's. Does the city carry them? Crush them? Ignore them? Does it mourn with them? Does it betray them? Does it stay behind while they evolve—or evolve too late?

Give the city motion. Even inertia is a kind of movement, when it costs something.

The skyline can change. The flood line can rise. The mural can get painted—or painted over. A character might see the place differently, even if the place hasn't moved. And sometimes the city doesn't just resist—it cracks open. Makes room. Leaves a corner unstamped, unwatched. And in that sliver, something new begins. Because in the end, fiction doesn't require resolution—only resonance.

In Summary: Write the City Like It's Watching

You've now built a toolkit for writing cities with emotional, political, and narrative force.

- You've learned to see the city as a character—with power, constraint, memory, and mood.
- You've learned to place your story where pressure gathers: at the edges, the thresholds, the seams.
- You've learned that setting isn't static. Cities shift. They wound. They resist. They call back what was buried.
- And you've learned that every block holds contradiction—and every silence holds weight.

Now, you know what to do with that.

Don't flatten cities into backdrops. Don't borrow what you won't name. Don't mistake mood for meaning. Instead:

- Write the systems beneath the surface.
- Write the memory in the brick.
- Write the character who walks through the city—and the city that walks through them.

Because when you write the city like it's alive, your fiction moves. And when you write it like it remembers, your fiction lasts.

Now go write a city that breathes. When you're done outlining, drafting, polishing—step back and ask: does the city breathe? Does it bruise, resist, seduce, protect, expose? Can you feel its rhythm under the dialogue, its pressure in the plot? If not, return to the street. The one with the flickering sign, the heat rising off the pavement, the rusted gate someone once slipped through. Let the city speak first. Then write what it won't let your characters forget.

And make sure it bites back.

Exercise 1: The City First

Prompt: You've likely written scenes by starting with a character or a conflict. Now flip it. Let the city be the first force—and build outward.

Step 1: Choose a city

It can be one you know well, one you've imagined, or one you've been circling but haven't yet claimed on the page.

Step 2: Assign it three defining qualities:

- **Emotional atmosphere** (e.g., brittle, suspicious, post-traumatic, euphoric, mercenary)
- **Physical constraint** (e.g., flood zones, elevated trains, checkpoint curfews, blinding wind)
- **Social tension** (e.g., redevelopment versus resistance, language erasure, visibility politics)

Step 3: Write a 1–2 page scene

No exposition. No context dump. Just drop a character into this city and let the place shape the tone, tension, and movement. Let the setting do emotional and narrative work. Let the constraint become pressure. Let the character want something the city isn't ready to give.

Optional challenge: End the scene with a spatial shift—crossing a threshold, opening a door, boarding a bus—that changes the emotional atmosphere entirely. Show how the city evolves within the span of a single encounter.

Sample Answer

- **City:** Chicago—winter, pre-election season, South Side
- **Emotional atmosphere:** Paranoid, weary, bracing
- **Physical constraint:** Bitter cold, buses running behind, sidewalks iced and half-shoveled
- **Social tension:** Grassroots organizing versus performative political visibility

Scene excerpt

Malik waits for the 63rd Street bus with his collar up and his knuckles jammed deep into his sleeves. A new billboard above the gas station reads *A Safer Chicago Starts With You*—bright, clean, off-center. No one looks up at it. A cop car idles with its lights off at the corner, engine humming like it's waiting for something to go wrong. He checks the time. He's late for canvassing, but the organizer told him not to worry—"We move on foot when we have to."

He steps off the curb, shoes skidding. He doesn't fall, but he hears someone behind him say, "Careful." The voice is warm. Familiar. A block he hasn't walked in five years suddenly tilts toward memory. He turns down it anyway. Cold in his teeth. Voice in his ear. Whatever he thought he wanted—he forgets.

Narrative takeaway: The emotional atmosphere (paranoia plus weariness), the physical cold, and the social tension between street presence and institutional performance all play through the scene's tone, pace, and unease.

Exercise 2: City-as-Character Profile

Prompt: Most writers sketch their protagonists—goals, wounds, fears, contradictions. Now, do the same for your city. Fill out the profile below—seriously, not symbolically. Treat it like a person you're about to put on the page.

Your city:

- ▸ Name:
- ▸ Apparent Age: (How old does it feel?)
- ▸ Dominant Mood: (Is it anxious? Confident? Desperate?)
- ▸ Deep Wound: (What hasn't healed? What does no one talk about?)
- ▸ Desire: (What is the city trying to become?)
- ▸ Public Mask: (What image does it sell to outsiders?)
- ▸ Private Truth: (What really drives it?)
- ▸ Who It Protects:
- ▸ Who It Punishes:
- ▸ How It Shows Affection:
- ▸ How It Withdraws:

Return to your story. Does your fiction reflect this version of the city—or a flattened one? Does it show how the city makes people feel safe, seen, threatened, displaced, obsessed, abandoned, alive? If not, consider revising until the city is legible—not just to the reader, but to itself.

Sample Answer

- ▸ **City:** Chicago
- ▸ **Apparent Age:** 80—but still clocking into work every morning like it's 1952
- ▸ **Dominant Mood:** Defensive
- ▸ **Deep Wound:** Public trust broken after repeated betrayals—from redlining to police torture to shuttered schools
- ▸ **Desire:** To be seen as "world-class" without reconciling with what it's buried
- ▸ **Public Mask:** Gritty but hopeful. Diverse. Resilient.
- ▸ **Private Truth:** Grief-ridden and afraid of being left behind
- ▸ **Who It Protects:** Developers, tourists, institutions

with names on buildings
- **Who It Punishes:** Those who stay too long in the wrong neighborhood without permission
- **How It Shows Affection:** Block parties, porch conversations, weather solidarity
- **How It Withdraws:** Quiet closures. Evictions. A chill in the wind that no one calls by name.

Narrative takeaway: A character operating in this Chicago isn't just shaped by weather and transit—they're navigating a city that both mourns and mythologizes itself, a place where silence is often survival.

About the Author

Bryan Nyary is a writer based in Chicago's Printers Row and holds a PhD in Creative Writing from Teesside University. His doctoral research explored how autobiographical fiction can offer narrative safety in the wake of trauma. His creative work is grounded in a deep fascination with the texture of urban space—its rhythms, ruptures, contradictions, tensions, and emotional weight. He writes fiction that treats cities not as scenery, but as agents of conflict, pressure, and transformation. His short fiction has appeared in various small press magazines, and his forthcoming novels include *Aidland* and *Windy City Couriers*. He believes stories live in the alleys and under the El tracks—where the light doesn't quite reach, and what's gone still lingers.